P9-AFA-567

# Quiltmaker's fancy

## 16 TRADITIONAL QUILTS FOR ALL SKILL LEVELS

From the Editors and Contributors of *Quiltmaker* Magazine

C&T PUBLISHING

Text and artwork copyright © 2007 CK Media

Publisher: Amy Marson

Editorial Director: Gailen Runge

Acquisitions Editor: Jan Grigsby

Editors: Lynn Koolish and Kesel Wilson

Technical Editor: Elin Thomas

Copyeditor: Stacy Chamness

Proofreader: Wordfirm Inc.

Book Designer: Susan H. Hartman

Cover Designer: Kristy Zacharias

Production Coordinator: Kirstie L. Pettersen

Photography: Mellisa Karlin Mahoney, unless otherwise noted

Published by C&T Publishing, Inc., P.O. Box 1456, Lafayette, CA 94549

All rights reserved. No part of this work covered by the copyright hereon may be used in any form or reproduced by any means—graphic, electronic, or mechanical, including photocopying, recording, taping, or information storage and retrieval systems—without written permission from the publisher. The copyrights on individual artworks are retained by the artists as noted in *Quiltmaker's Fancy*. These designs may be used to make items only for personal use or donation to nonprofit groups for sale. Each piece of finished merchandise for sale must carry a conspicuous label with the following information: Designs copyright © 2007 CK Media from the book *Quiltmaker's Fancy* from C&T Publishing, Inc.

Attention Copy Shops: Please note the following exception—publisher and author give permission to photocopy pages 7, 10, 11, 20, 25, 26, 30, 31, 43, 47, 51–53, 57, 58, 62, 63, 67, 68, 72, and 73 for personal use only.

Attention Teachers: C&T Publishing, Inc., encourages you to use this book as a text for teaching. Contact us at 800-284-1114 or www.ctpub.com for more information about the C&T Teachers Program.

We take great care to ensure that the information included in our products is accurate and presented in good faith, but no warranty is provided nor are results guaranteed. Having no control over the choices of materials or procedures used, neither the author nor C&T Publishing, Inc., shall have any liability to any person or entity with respect to any loss or damage caused directly or indirectly by the information contained in this book. For your convenience, we post an up-to-date listing of corrections on our website (www.ctpub.com). If a correction is not already noted, please contact our customer service department at ctinfo@ctpub.com or at P.O. Box 1456, Lafayette, CA 94549.

Trademark (™) and registered trademark (®) names are used throughout this book. Rather than use the symbols with every occurrence of a trademark or registered trademark name, we are using the names only in the editorial fashion and to the benefit of the owner, with no intention of infringement.

Library of Congress Cataloging-in-Publication Data

Quiltmaker's fancy : 16 traditional quilts for all skill levels / from the editors and contributors of Quiltmaker magazine.

　　p. cm.

　Includes bibliographical references.

　ISBN-13: 978-1-57120-447-9 (paper trade : alk. paper)

　ISBN-10: 1-57120-447-4 (paper trade : alk. paper)

　1. Patchwork. 2. Quilting. 3. Patchwork quilts. I. Quiltmaker magazine. II. Title.

TT835.Q5477 2007

746.46'041--dc22

2007007740

Printed in China

10 9 8 7 6 5 4 3 2 1

# Contents

## PREFACE

Comfort… home… love. Nothing says these things quite like a cozy traditional quilt. Maybe that's why we never get tired of the old favorites.

Our love of traditional quilts inspired us to put together this collection of designs that were originally published in the pages of *Quiltmaker*. If you're like us, your house is already full of quilts you've made, or found at yard sales or second-hand shops, or received as gifts. But there's always room for a few more! This timeless collection includes some of our very favorites.

The design inspirations for these quilts came from many places: vintage quilts bought in second-hand stores, blocks inherited from another quilter, museum collections, beautiful vintage fabrics, even a child's doodle on her homework! The Goose Track blocks in *Too Many Geese*, came to Linda Foster when she saw a flock of geese standing in a parking lot. Turid Margaret Uren started *Country Roses* as a hand-piecing exercise while she worked as a traffic controller for helicopters and vessels on an offshore oil rig in the North Sea. Anne Olsen made *Rising Sun* from blocks originally pieced by an unknown quilter back in the 1930s. Anne rebuilt the blocks in new colors and turned them into a beautiful quilt.

Some of these quilts are pieced, some appliquéd, and some a happy mixture of both techniques. There are designs at every level, from easy to challenging. Most come with instructions for making at least two sizes, so you can adapt them to a variety of uses.

Along with the projects, you'll also find a wealth of helpful tips on uses of color, rotary cutting, assembly, quilting motifs, and much more—a veritable minicourse on quilting.

So, happy quilting! We hope you'll enjoy making, using, and giving these quilts as much as we enjoyed bringing them to you.

*Brenda Groelz*, Editor-in-Chief,
*Quiltmaker* magazine

# Sarah's garden

Designed and made by Shirley Wegert,
Englewood, Colorado.

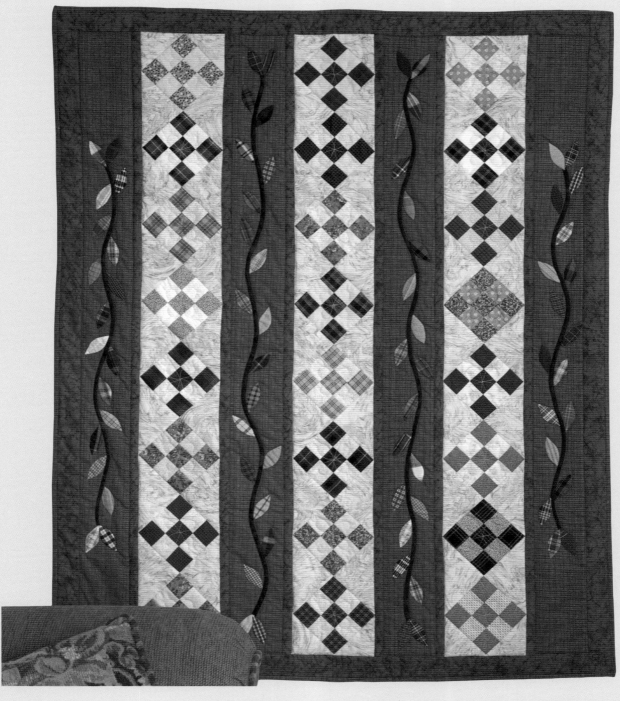

n quilt history books, Shirley saw a number of strippy vine quilts. Since she loved making scrappy Nine Patches, she joined these two ideas to make this quilt for a friend.

## MATERIALS AND CUTTING

| QUILT SIZE: | Crib/Wall Quilt |
|---|---|
| | 43″ × 54½″ |
| **BLOCK SIZE:** | |
| 4½″ | |
| **YARDAGE:** (44″ fabric) | |
| **Cream Prints** | ⅞ yard |
| | 12 B, 42 C |
| | 24 scraps |
| per scrap | 4 A |
| **Brown Plaid** | 1⅔ yards |
| sashes* | 4 at 5½″ × 54½″ |
| double-fold binding | 5 at 2¼″ × 45″ |
| **Dark Green Print** | ⅝ yard |
| bias strips | 7 at 1¼″ × 26″ |
| **Medium Green Print** | 1⅔ yards |
| border**   sides | 2 at 2¼″ × 53½″ |
|      top/bottom | 2 at 2¼″ × 45½″ |
| strips* & ** | 6 at 1¼″ × 53½″ |
| **Assorted Prints/Plaids** | 24 scraps |
| per scrap | 5 A |
| | 78 scraps |
| per scrap | 1 D |
| **Backing** | 3 yards |
| panels | 2 at 30″ × 47″ |
| sleeve | 1 at 9″ × 43″ |
| **Batting** | 47″ × 59″ |

\* Trim the sashes to 4½″ × 51½″ after the appliqué is complete.

\*\* An extra 2″ has been added to the length for insurance.

## ABOUT THIS QUILT

*For help with all phases of the quiltmaking process, see Quilting Basics (pages 74–78).*

One plaid was used for the sashes and binding, but the leaves use many plaid scraps. A vine was added to each sash, and the leaves were appliquéd in a random placement.

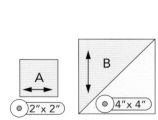

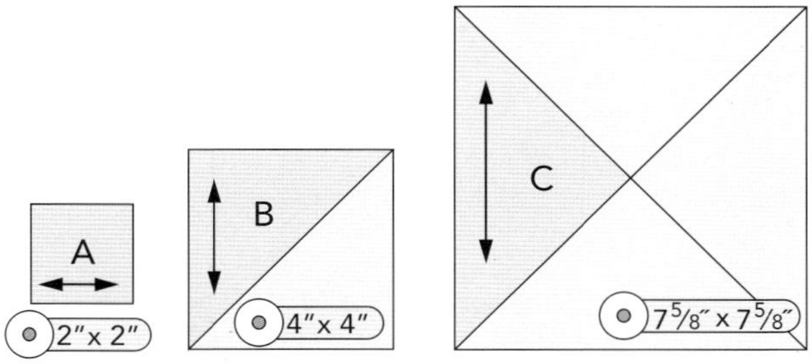

Align arrows with lengthwise or crosswise grain of fabric. A corner-trimming template and directions for using it are in Quilting Basics.

## MAKING AND JOINING THE BLOCKS

**1** Following the diagram below, make the blocks. Press the seam allowances as shown.

**2** Referring to the center pieced row on the assembly diagram (page 7), sew the blocks, B's, and C's together to make 3 vertical rows. Press the seam allowances as shown.

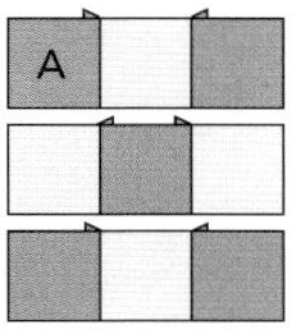

Block Piecing, make 24.

*Sarah's Garden*    5

## APPLIQUÉING THE SASHES

**1** Join the bias strips to make one long strip. Prepare this strip for appliqué following the steps in the Bias Strips section of Quilting Basics (page 76), *sewing ⅜″ from the fold.*

**2** Cut the strip into 2 stems 31″ long for the Sash 1's and 2 stems 46″ long for the Sash 2's.

**3** Prepare the leaves for appliqué using your favorite method. If you plan to hand appliqué, see *A New Tack*, below.

**4** Fold each Sash 1 in half end-to-end and lightly press the midpoint. Fold the bias stem in half and crease its center, also.

**5** Following the Sash 1 appliqué placement diagram, match centers and pin the stem in place. Appliqué the stem and then add the leaves (D patches). Repeat these steps to complete the remaining Sash 1 and Sash 2's. Centering the appliqué, trim each Sash 1 and Sash 2 to 4½″ × 51½″.

## JOINING THE ROWS

**1** Matching centers, sew the medium green strips to one side of the Sash 1's and both sides of the Sash 2's. Trim any excess length even with the sashes. Press the seam allowances toward the medium green strips.

**2** Starting with the center row, match centers and ends. Pin a Sash 2 unit along the length of the row, easing in any fullness as needed. Sew together. Press the seam allowances toward the medium green strip. Repeat these steps to join the remaining sash units and rows as shown in the Assembly diagram (page 7).

## ADDING THE SQUARED BORDER

Sew the side border strips to the quilt and press the seam allowances toward the strips. Trim the extra length even with the quilt edges. Add the top and bottom strips in the same way.

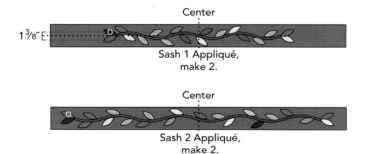

Center

1³/₈″ E

D

Sash 1 Appliqué,
make 2.

Center

D

Sash 2 Appliqué,
make 2.

## A NEW TACK

The *tack stitch* is a nondecorative appliqué stitch that is quick and easy. Thread the needle with 18″–24″ of thread in a color that matches your patch. Begin the stitch by coming up from the background, catching the turn-under allowance and the patch. Then bring the needle back down through the background, over the folded edge of the patch and just under the fold. Gently tug the stitch with a forward motion. Begin your next stitch 1/16″–1/8″ away from the first stitch.

Cross
Section

Tack Stitch

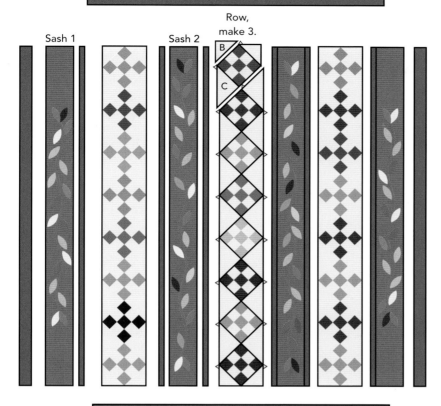

Sash 1

Sash 2

Row, make 3.

B

C

Assembly

# QUILTING AND FINISHING

**1** Trace the **Floret Quilting** and mark a motif in each block.

**2** Layer and baste together the backing, batting, and quilt top.

**3** Quilt the blocks, rows, sashes, and appliqué in the ditch, then quilt the marked motifs.

**4** Bind the quilt.

**5** If you would like to hang your quilt on a wall, add a sleeve to the backing.

Quilting Placement

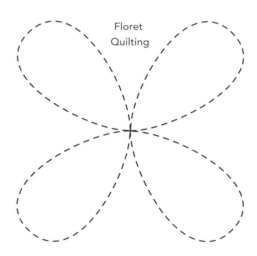

Floret Quilting

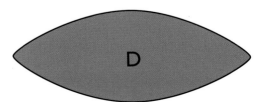

D

Add ³⁄₁₆˝ turn-under allowance to D.

# Log cabin star

Designed and made by Joyce Luff,
Denver, Colorado.

I n Mary Ellen Hopkins' *A Log Cabin Notebook,* she refers to a Log Cabin block as a right triangle. Intrigued, Joyce found a block layout in the book that inspired her. Joyce didn't want a large quilt, so she made her blocks very small.

MATERIALS AND CUTTING

| QUILT SIZE: | Wall Quilt |
| --- | --- |
| | 43″ × 43″ |
| **FINISHED BLOCK:** | |
| 2¾″ | |
| **YARDAGE:** (44″ fabric) | |
| **White Print** | 1 yard |
| | 4 A, 4 B, 8 C, 4 D, 4 E |
| **Value #1 (lightest)** | ¼ yard |
| strips | 2 at 1″ × 40″ |
| strips | 2 at 1½″ × 40″ |
| **Value #2** | ⅝ yard |
| strips | 8 at 1″ × 40″ |
| strips | 7 at 1½″ × 40″ |
| **Value #3** | ⅝ yard |
| strips | 8 at 1″ × 40″ |
| strips | 7 at 1½″ × 40″ |
| **Value #4** | 1⅛ yards |
| strips | 16 at 1″ × 40″ |
| strips | 13 at 1½″ × 40″ |
| **Value #5** | ⅔ yard |
| strips | 9 at 1″ × 40″ |
| strips | 8 at 1½″ × 40″ |
| **Value #6** | ⅝ yard |
| strips | 8 at 1″ × 40″ |
| strips | 7 at 1½″ × 40″ |
| **Value #7 (darkest)** | ⅓ yard |
| strips | 3 at 1″ × 40″ |
| strips | 3 at 1½″ × 40″ |
| **Dark Pink Print** | ⅛ yard |
| strips | 3 at 1″ × 40″ |
| **Dark Multiprint** | ⅜ yard |
| double-fold binding | 5 at 2¼″ × 40″ |
| **Stripe** | 1⅜ yards |
| border strips* | 4 at 2¾″ × 45½″ |
| **Backing** | 2⅞ yards |
| panels | 2 at 24″ × 47″ |
| sleeve | 1 at 9″ × 43″ |
| **Batting** | 47″ × 47″ |

\* An extra 2″ has been added to the length for insurance.
Yardage amounts are generous for the foundation-piecing technique.

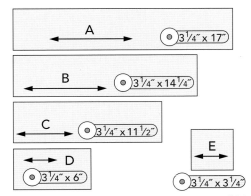

Align arrows with lengthwise or crosswise grain of fabric.

A — 3¼″ × 17″

B — 3¼″ × 14¼″

C — 3¼″ × 11½″

D — 3¼″ × 6″

E — 3¼″ × 3¼″

## ABOUT THIS QUILT

*For help with all phases of the quiltmaking process, including foundation piecing and mitered borders, see Quilting Basics (pages 74–78).*

For this quilt, many scraps were separated into seven different values. You can make this quilt any color you desire; however, make sure that the seven fabrics you choose are distinct lights, mediums, and darks. The yardage box and block diagrams identify the values by number rather than color—#1 being the lightest and #7 the darkest. You'll notice that we've listed strip measurements in the yardage box. Using strips for the foundation patches is efficient—just sew and trim.

The 1″-wide strips are for Patches 1–9, and the 1½″-wide strips are for Patches 10–13. Patch 1, the "chimney," uses the same dark pink print in all the blocks.

## MAKING THE CABINS

1 Make 108 copies of the foundation pattern (page 10). The diagrams below identify which value numbers are needed for each block.

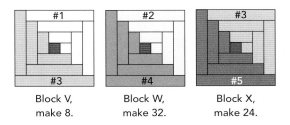

Block V, make 8.    Block W, make 32.    Block X, make 24.

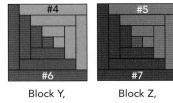

Block Y, make 32.    Block Z, make 12.

## TIP

Use a size 90/14 needle in your sewing machine and set your stitch length to 18–20 (1.5 metric) stitches to the inch. The larger needle and shorter stitches make tearing away foundation paper easier.

**2** Following the numerical sequence, foundation piece each block. Trim the excess fabric and foundation paper on the outer line.

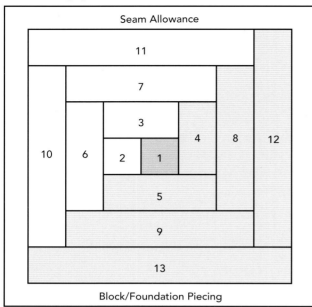

Seam Allowance

Block/Foundation Piecing

Pattern is the reverse
of the finished block.

## ASSEMBLING THE TOP

**1** Referring to the Assembly diagram, sew the blocks and patches together for each row. Press the seam allowances of every other row in the same direction. Join the rows.

**2** Carefully remove the foundation paper and press the seam allowances in the same direction.

## ADDING THE MITERED BORDER

Matching centers, sew the border strips to the quilt top. Miter each corner, trim the seam allowances to ¼", and press open.

## QUILTING AND FINISHING

**1** Trace the ½ **Cabin Feathers Quilting** (page 11) and dotted placement line onto tracing paper. Flip the tracing, align, and mark again to complete the motif. Matching adjacent edges of the quilt top, fold and lightly crease the corners.

**2** Align the placement line on the fold and mark a motif in each corner.

**3** Layer and baste together the backing, batting, and quilt top.

**4** Quilt the blocks in the ditch and the diagonal lines as shown. Quilt the marked motifs.

**5** Bind the quilt.

**6** To display *Log Cabin Star* on a wall, sew a sleeve to the backing by hand.

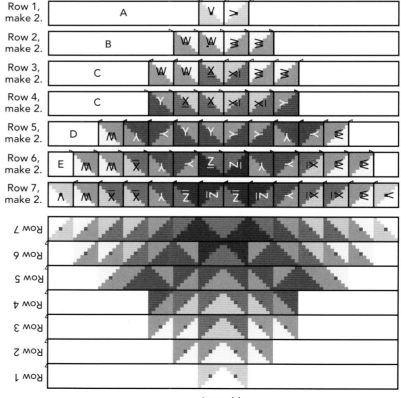

Assembly

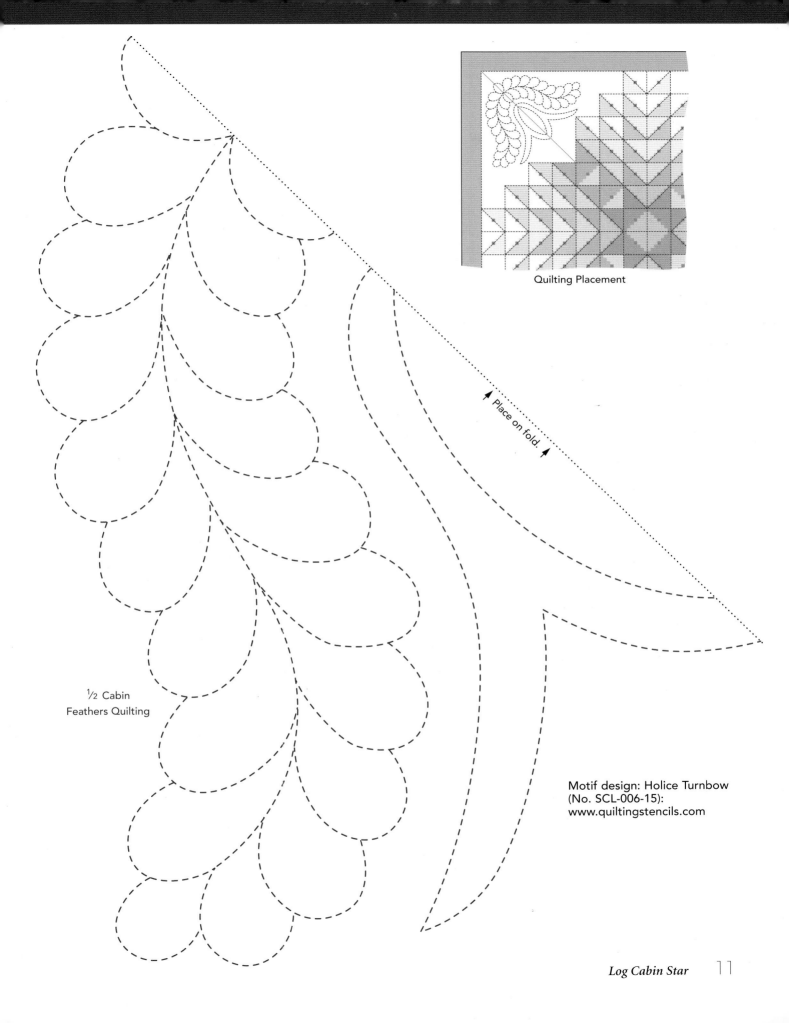

Quilting Placement

Place on fold.

½ Cabin
Feathers Quilting

Motif design: Holice Turnbow
(No. SCL-006-15):
www.quiltingstencils.com

# 9×9×9

**Designed and made by Theresa Eisinger.**

The small Nine Patches were the result of a block exchange begun on September 9, 1999 (9/9/99). Theresa added dark and light frames and created larger Nine Patches from small ones set 3 × 3, then arranged these blocks into one big Nine Patch for the quilt center.

EASY

## MATERIALS AND CUTTING

| QUILT SIZE: | Topper (shown) | Crib/Wall Quilt |
|---|---|---|
| | 77½" × 77½" | 49½" × 49½" |
| **FINISHED BLOCK:** | | |
| 16½" | | |
| **YARDAGE:** (44" fabric) | | |
| **Dark Brown Print** | 1⅛ yards | 1 yard |
| double-fold binding | 9 at 2¼" × 39" | 6 at 2¼" × 38" |
| | 50 B, 50 C | 50 B, 50 C |
| **Brown Plaid** | ⅜ yard | none for this size |
| | 28 B, 28 C | |
| **Tan Print** | 2½ yards | ⅝ yard |
| border 3 strips*    sides | 2 at 5½" × 70" | none for this size |
| top/bottom | 2 at 5½" × 80" | none for this size |
| | 10 D, 10 E | 10 D, 10 E |
| **Light Tan Print** | ½ yard | ½ yard |
| | 40 B, 40 C | 40 B, 40 C |
| **Cream Print 1** | ⅝ yard | ⅝ yard |
| | 8 D, 8 E | 8 D, 8 E |
| **Cream Print 2** | ⅝ yard | none for this size |
| | 56 B, 56 C | |
| **Dark Blue Print** | ½ yard | ½ yard |
| | 40 B, 40 C | 40 B, 40 C |
| **Medium Blue Print** | ⅜ yard | none for this size |
| | 28 B, 28 C | |
| **Light Blue Print** | ⅜ yard | ⅜ yard |
| | 32 B, 32 C | 32 B, 32 C |
| **Multiprint** | 1⅞ yards | none for this size |
| border 1 strips**    sides | 2 at 5" × 50" | |
| top/bottom | 2 at 5" × 59" | |
| **Assorted Dark Prints**   a total of 1¼ [⅞] yard(s) | 137 scraps | 81 scraps |
| from each scrap | 5 A | 5 A |
| **Assorted Light Prints**   a total of 1⅛ [⅔] yard(s) | 137 scraps | 81 scraps |
| from each scrap | 4 A | 4 A |
| **Backing** | 4⅞ yards | 3¼ yards |
| panels | 2 at 42" × 82" | 2 at 28" × 54" |
| sleeve | none for this size | 1 at 9" × 49" |
| **Batting** | 82" × 82" | 54" × 54" |

\* An extra 2" has been added to the length for insurance.

\*\* Seam allowance is included in the length, but no extra has been added for insurance.

## ABOUT THIS QUILT

*For help with all phases of the quiltmaking process, see Quilting Basics (pages 74–78).*

Directions are for both the topper and the crib/wall quilt. Both sizes include the nine-block center; the topper has three additional borders. Information specific to the crib/wall size is given in brackets.

Each Nine Patch is made with 5 dark A's and 4 light A's. The fabrics framing the Nine Patches (B's and C's) alternate in value to repeat the Nine Patch theme. The fabrics chosen for the D's and E's in the Y and Z blocks alternate in value, repeating the theme yet again.

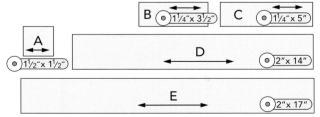

Align arrows with lengthwise or crosswise grain of fabric.

# MAKING THE BLOCKS

**1** Following the diagrams for value placement, piece the Nine Patches and then piece the units. Press the seam allowances as shown.

Nine Patch
Piecing,
make 137 [81].

Unit 1 Piecing,
make 25 [25].

Unit 2,
make 20 [20].

Unit 3,
make 20 [20].

Unit 4,
make 16 [16].

Unit 5,
make 14 [0].

Unit 6,
make 28 [0].

Unit 7,
make 14 [0].

**2** Orienting the units as shown (to avoid the bulk of stacked seam allowances), join the Unit 1's, Unit 2's, D, and E patches to make the Y blocks. Join the Unit 3's, Unit 4's, D, and E patches to make the Z blocks.

**3** Join the blocks as shown in the Assembly diagram to make the rows. Press the seam allowances toward the Z blocks.

**4** Join the rows and press these seam allowances in one direction. If you are making the crib/wall quilt, go to Quilting and Finishing.

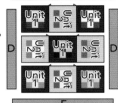

Block Y Piecing,
make 5 [5].

Block Z,
make 4 [4].

# ADDING THE SQUARED BORDERS

**1** For the topper only, matching centers and ends, sew the border 1 side strips to the quilt, easing any fullness if necessary. Press the seam allowances toward the strips. Add the top and bottom strips in the same way.

**2** Construct 56 Unit 5's, 6's and 7's and, referring to the Assembly diagram, join them to make the border 2 strips.

**3** Matching centers and ends, sew the border 2 side strips to the quilt and press seam allowances toward border 1. Repeat for the top and bottom border 2 strips.

**4** Sew the border 3 side strips to the quilt. Press the seam allowances away from the quilt center and trim any extra length. Add the border 3 top and bottom strips in the same way.

# QUILTING AND FINISHING

**1** Mark a 3″ diameter circle and 4½″ scallop in the Z blocks (and in borders 2 and 3 for the topper) following the portion(s) of the Quilting Placement diagram that you need. Mark the arc shown in red by eye.

**2** Layer the backing, batting, and the quilt top and baste the layers together.

**3** Using the patchwork as a guide, quilt a diagonal grid as shown and quilt the marked motifs.

**4** Bind the quilt. [Sew a sleeve to the backing by hand to display the wall quilt.]

Quilting Placement

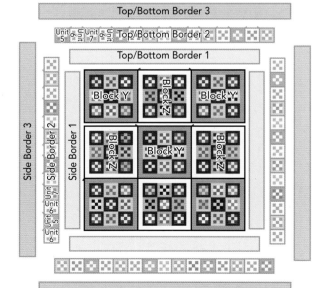

Assembly
Crib/wall quilt is shown in darker colors.
Topper includes the complete diagram.

# Friendship twist

**Designed by Kellie and Erin Wilcoxon.
Made by Cindy Erickson. Fabrics from
Red Rooster Fabrics and RJR Fabrics.**

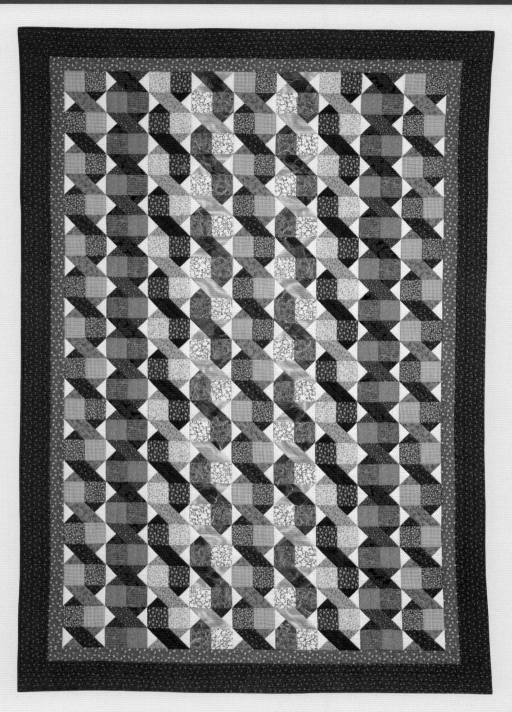

While reviewing homework for her nine-year-old daughter, Kellie, Erin noticed a doodle on her paper that could make an interesting quilt block. With a little modification, she came up with this design. Just goes to show, you're never too old to learn from your children.

EASY

## MATERIALS AND CUTTING

| QUILT SIZE: | | Long Twin Comforter (shown) | King Comforter |
|---|---|---|---|
| | | 66″ × 96″ | 104″ × 98″ |
| **FINISHED BLOCK:** 6″ × 12″ | | | |
| **YARDAGE:** (44″ fabric) | | | |
| **Dark Blue, Dark Teal, Dark Lime, Dark Brown, Dark Gold & Dark Red** | | ⅜ yard each | ¾ yard each |
| from each | | 28 A, 14 B | 56 A, 28 B |
| **Light Blue, Light Teal, Light Lime, Light Brown, Light Gold & Light Red** | | ⅜ yard each | ⅔ yard each |
| from each | strips for bands | 3 at 3½″ × 40″ | 6 at 3½″ × 35″ |
| **Dark Green Print** | | 2¾ yards | 3¼ yards |
| border 2 strips* | sides | 2 at 4½″ × 90½″ | 2 at 5½″ × 90½″ |
| | top/bottom | 2 at 4½″ × 68½″ | 2 at 5½″ × 106½″ |
| double-fold binding | | 4 at 2¼″ × 87″ | 5 at 2¼″ × 86″ |
| | | 42 A, 21 B | 42 A, 21 B |
| **Light Green & Light Tan** | | ½ yard each | ½ yard each |
| from each | strips for bands | 4 at 3½″ × 40″ | 4 at 3½″ × 40″ |
| **Dark Tan Print** | | ⅝ yard | ⅝ yard |
| | | 42 A, 21 B | 42 A, 21 B |
| **Tan Multiprint**** | | 2⅝ yards | 3 yards |
| border 1 strips* | sides | 2 at 2½″ × 86½″ | 2 at 2½″ × 86½″ |
| | top/bottom | 2 at 2½″ × 60½″ | 2 at 2½″ × 96½″ |
| **Cream Print** | | 1 yard | 1⅝ yards |
| | | 252 A | 420 A |
| **Backing** | | 6 yards | 9 yards |
| panels | | 2 at 36″ × 100″ | 3 at 37″ × 102″ |
| **Batting** | | 70″ × 100″ | 108″ × 102″ |

* An extra 2″ has been added to the length for insurance.

** If you prefer to piece the border 1 strips, you'll need only ⅔ [⅞] yard. Cut 8 [10] 2½-wide strips and join them. Cut this strip to the required border 1 lengths.

## About This Quilt

*For help with all phases of the quiltmaking process, see Quilting Basics (pages 74–78).*

Directions are for both the long twin comforter and the king comforter. Information specific to the king size is given in brackets.

Notice that each twist is made with four fabrics, a light and a dark version of two different colors. To cut the B patches, first cut a strip 3½″ wide and trim the end as shown; then cut patches 2⅝″ wide. Repeat to cut the number of B's listed for each fabric in the yardage box.

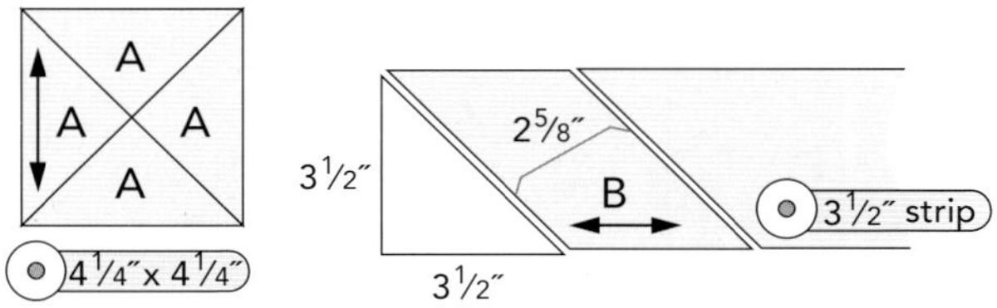

A
A
A
A
4¼″x 4¼″
3½″
2⅝″
B
3½″
3½″ strip


Align arrows with lengthwise or crosswise grain of fabric. A corner-trimming template and directions for using it are in Quilting Basics.

## Making the Blocks

**1** Sew the strips together to make the Band A's, B's, C's, and D's. Cut the bands at 3½″ intervals to make the Unit 1's, 2's, 3's, and 4's.

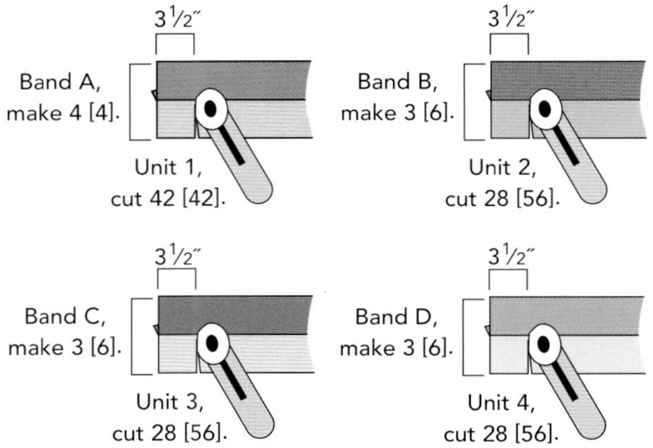

3½″
Band A, make 4 [4].
Unit 1, cut 42 [42].
3½″
Band B, make 3 [6].
Unit 2, cut 28 [56].
3½″
Band C, make 3 [6].
Unit 3, cut 28 [56].
3½″
Band D, make 3 [6].
Unit 4, cut 28 [56].

**2** Join the units and patches to make the Block W's, X's, Y's, and Z's.

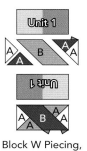

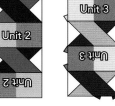

Block W Piecing, make 21 [21].

Block X, make 14 [28].

Block Y, make 14 [28].

Block Z, make 14 [28].

## ASSEMBLING THE TOP

**1** Referring to the Assembly diagram, join the blocks to make the rows. Sew the rows together in the order shown.

**2** Sew the border 1 side strips to the quilt. After pressing, trim any extra length. In the same way, add the top and bottom strips. Repeat to add the border 2 strips.

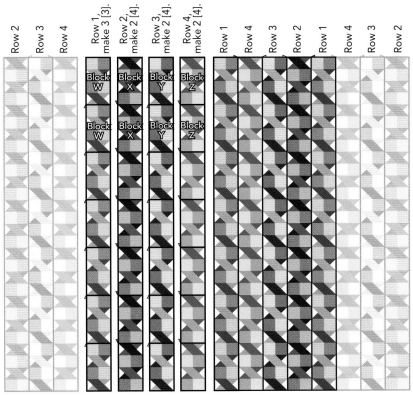

Assembly
Long twin comforter is shown in darker colors.
King comforter includes the complete diagram.

## QUILTING AND FINISHING

**1** Referring to the Quilting Placement diagram, mark a line through the center of each twist.

**2** Layer and baste together the backing, batting, and the quilt top.

**3** For each row, quilt the "twists" in the ditch and quilt the marked lines. To quilt by machine, see the diagram for continuous-line quilting; for each row, start at the dot and follow the arrows. Quilt the borders in the ditch. In border 2, quilt 2 parallel lines.

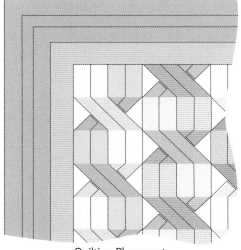

Quilting Placement

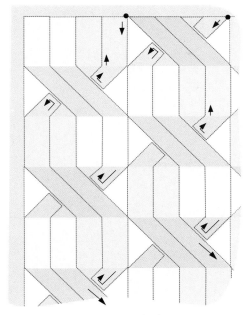

Continuous-Line Quilting

**4** Bind the quilt.

# Hattie's choice

Designed and made by Sherry Bain Driver.
Quilted by J. Renée Howell.
Backing fabric from Robert Kaufmann.

Designed as a mystery quilt for a state-wide guild, this simplified version of the traditional Farmer's Daughter block uses quick techniques and easy-to-make units. Add a casual approach to machine quilting and you'll have your quilt finished in no time!

## MATERIALS AND CUTTING

| QUILT SIZE: | | Twin Comforter (shown) | Queen Comforter |
|---|---|---|---|
| | | 66″ × 90″ | 94″ × 94″ |
| **FINISHED BLOCK:** | | | |
| 10″ | | | |
| **YARDAGE:** (44″ fabric) | | | |
| **Red Print** | | 1¼ yards | 1⅞ yards |
| strips for bands | | 15 at 2½″ × 40″ | 23 at 2½″ × 40″ |
| | | 24 B | 28 B |
| **Light Gold Solid** | | ½ yard | ¾ yard |
| | | 96 B | 144 B |
| **Gold Print** | | 1½ yards | 2⅛ yards |
| | | 96 A, 35 B | 144 A, 49 B |
| **Brown and Gold Stripe** | | 1¼ yards* | 1¼ yards |
| strips for bands | | 4 at 6½″ × 40″ | 6 at 6½″ × 40″ |
| **Brown Check** | | ⅔ yard | ⅞ yard |
| double-fold binding | | 9 at 2¼″ × 39″ | 11 at 2¼″ × 38″ |
| **Brown Print** | | 2⅜ yards | 2¾ yards |
| border 1 strips** | sides | 2 at 6½″ × 80½″ | 2 at 6½″ × 80½″ |
| | top/bottom | 2 at 6½″ × 68½″ | 2 at 6½″ × 92½″ |
| | | 4 B, 20 C | 4 B, 24 C |
| **Dark Brown Print** | | 1½ yards | 3⅝ yards |
| border 2 strips** | sides | none for this size | 2 at 2½″ × 92½″ |
| | top/bottom | none for this size | 2 at 2½″ × 96½″ |
| strips for bands | | 8 at 2½″ × 40″ | 13 at 2½″ × 40″ |
| | | 192 B | 288 B |
| **Backing** | | 5⅝ yards | 8⅝ yards |
| panels | | 2 at 36″ × 94″ | 3 at 34″ × 98″ |
| **Batting** | | 70″ × 94″ | 98″ × 98″ |

\* This yardage is for a stripe that runs parallel to the selvages; for a non-stripe fabric, only ⅞ yard is needed. Requirement for the queen size remains the same.

\*\* An extra 2″ has been added to the length for insurance.

## ABOUT THIS QUILT

*For help with all phases of the quiltmaking process, see Quilting Basics (pages 74–78).*

Directions are for both the twin and the queen comforters. Information specific to the queen size is given in brackets.

This quilt was machine quilted from the backing side following designs in the print.

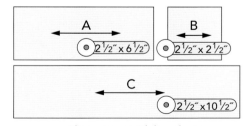

A   2½″ × 6½″

B   2½″ × 2½″

C   2½″ × 10½″

Align arrows with lengthwise or crosswise grain of fabric.

## MAKING THE BLOCKS AND SASHES

1 Join the strips to make the Band A's, B's, and C's. Cut these bands at 2½″ increments to make the Unit 1's, Unit 2's, and the sashes. Set the sashes aside.

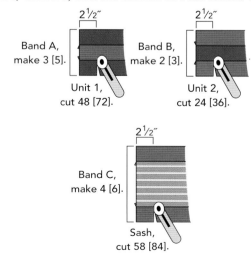

2½″

Band A, make 3 [5].

Unit 1, cut 48 [72].

2½″

Band B, make 2 [3].

Unit 2, cut 24 [36].

2½″

Band C, make 4 [6].

Sash, cut 58 [84].

**2** To make a stitch-and-flip Unit 3, align a brown print B patch with the edges of A, right sides together. Sew from corner to corner as shown. Trim the seam allowances to ¼", open B, and press. Repeat with another B where shown. Make 96 [144] Unit 3's.

Stitch & Flip

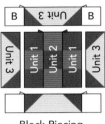

Unit 3,
make 96 [144].

**3** Join the light gold B's and Unit 1's, 2's, and 3's to make the blocks.

Block Piecing,
make 24 [36].

## ASSEMBLING THE TOP

**1** Following the assembly diagram, join brown print and red print B's and the C patches to make the Row 1's. For the Row 2's, join red print and gold print B's, and sashes. To make the Row 3's, join C's, sashes, and blocks. Sew the rows together in the order shown.

**2** Sew the border 1 side strips to the quilt. After pressing, trim any extra length. Repeat to add the border 1 top and bottom strips. [Add the border 2 strips in the same way.]

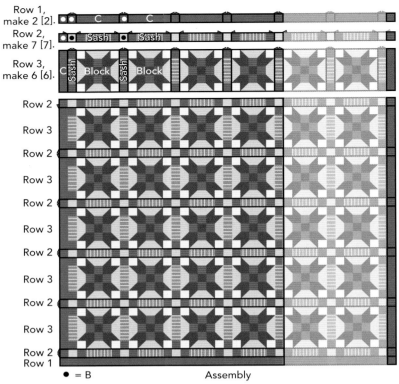

Row 1, make 2 [2].
Row 2, make 7 [7].
Row 3, make 6 [6].
Row 2
Row 3
Row 2
Row 3
Row 2
Row 3
Row 2
Row 3
Row 2
Row 3
Row 2
Row 1

● = B

Assembly

Twin comforter is shown in darker colors.
Queen comforter includes the complete diagram.

Hattie's
Garden Quilting

## QUILTING AND FINISHING

If the backing you have chosen does not have a print appropriate for quilting, use the **Hattie's Garden Quilting** motif (page 20).

See the *Free-Motion Quilting* tip for more information on machine quilting.

1 **For the bobbin quilting:** Pin or tape the quilt top right side down on a flat surface. Add the batting and the backing, then baste the layers together. Quilt, following the designs in the backing fabric. If necessary, connect the motifs with curvy lines.

2 **For the marked quilting:** Mark the **Hattie's Garden Quilting** randomly across the quilt top. Layer and baste together the backing, batting, and the quilt top. Quilt the marked motifs, connecting them with vines and leaves as shown in red.

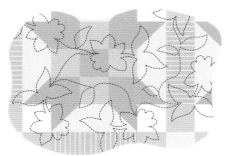

Quilting Placement

3 Bind the quilt.

Discover some handy products for machine quilting at quiltmaker.com.

## FREE-MOTION QUILTING

Free-motion machine quilting allows you to quilt in any direction without the machine's feed dogs guiding the quilt sandwich. With free-motion techniques, you can quilt curves and elaborate motifs—or even your signature—by machine, without turning your quilt.

For this technique, first lower or cover the machine's feed dogs and attach a darning foot or free-motion foot. Since the machine's feed dogs are not engaged, you'll maneuver the quilt under the needle using your hands. Your hand movements determine the direction and the size of the stitches. To make even-length stitches, run the machine at a consistent speed and make smooth hand movements. If the stitches are too long, slow down the quilt's movement and/or speed up the machine. Conversely, if the stitches are too short, slow the machine and/or move the quilt faster. Experiment until you find comfortable hand and machine speeds to create the stitch size you prefer.

With each stitch, the top and bobbin threads should lock in the batting layer so that no bobbin thread is pulled to the top and no top thread shows from the backing side. Unless you are using a specialty thread in the bobbin, these adjustments can usually be made by changing only the top tension. Turning the dial to a smaller number loosens the tension. For dials without numbers, remember, "Righty Tighty; Lefty Loosey."

Remember that improvement comes with practice. Relax, sew, and enjoy!

# Every
**Designed and made by Caroline Reardon.
Quilted by J. Reneé Howell.**

which way

This quilt, designed as a millennium quilt, uses more than 2000 different fabrics. Caroline began with blocks in a straight set, but as the piecing progressed, she liked the blocks better on point. That meant purchasing another cream print for the side triangles. Then she wanted a larger quilt, so she added borders in another closely matching cream. You'll be glad to know we're patterning it with just one cream print!

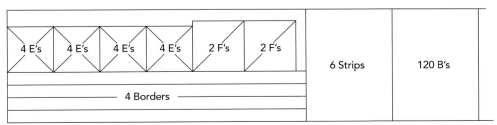

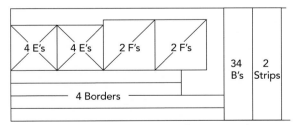

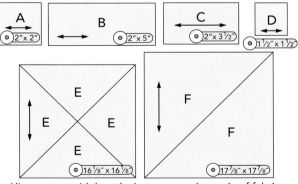

**MATERIALS AND CUTTING** · **INTERMEDIATE**

| QUILT SIZE: | | King Comforter (shown) | Sofa Quilt |
|---|---|---|---|
| | | 101½″ × 101½″ | 56⅞″ × 71¾″ |
| **FINISHED BLOCK:** | | | |
| 7½″ | | | |
| **YARDAGE:** (44″ fabric) | | | |
| **Cream Print*** | | 5⅛ yards | 2⅞ yards |
| border strips** | sides | 4 at 4½″ × 104″ | 2 at 4½″ × 74¼″ |
| | top/bottom | | 2 at 4½″ × 59⅜″ |
| strips for bands | | 6 at 5″ × 40″ | 2 at 5″ × 40″ |
| | | 120 B, 16 E, 4 F | 34 B, 6 E, 4 F |
| **Gold Print** | | 1 yard | ⅜ yard |
| | | 288 A | 96 A |
| **Light Purple Print** | | 1 yard | ⅜ yard |
| strips for bands | | 12 at 2″ × 40″ | 4 at 2″ × 40″ |
| | | 24 A | 14 A |
| **Assorted Purple Prints** | | ⅞ yard | ⅜ yard |
| | | 144 C | 48 C |
| **Purple Print** | | ⅞ yard | ⅝ yard |
| double-fold binding | | 12 at 2¼″ × 38″ | 8 at 2¼″ × 37″ |
| **Assorted Light Prints** | | 4¾ yards | 1⅝ yards |
| | | 1360 A, 369 D | 420 A, 128 D |
| **Assorted Dark Prints** | | 4⅝ yards | 1⅝ yards |
| | | 300 A, 560 C, 360 D | 85 A, 176 C, 124 D |
| **Backing** | | 9½ yards | 3⅝ yards |
| panels | | 3 at 36″ × 106″ | 2 at 39″ × 61″ |
| **Batting** | | 106″ × 106″ | 61″ × 76″ |

* Follow the cutting diagram below for best use of fabric.
** An extra 2″ has been added to the length for insurance.

## ABOUT THIS QUILT

*For help with all phases of the quiltmaking process, including mitered borders and blindstitching, see Quilting Basics (pages 74–78).*

Directions are for both the king comforter and a sofa quilt. Information specific to the sofa size is given in brackets.

For the sashes, each Flying Geese 1 is of one dark print and one light print. If you wish to follow this plan, cut two A's from each of 560 [176] assorted light prints and use this pair with a dark C for each Flying Geese 1.

Align arrows with lengthwise or crosswise grain of fabric. A corner-trimming template and directions for using it are in Quilting Basics.

Sofa Quilt Cutting Diagram for Cream Fabric

King Comforter Cutting Diagram for Cream Fabric

# MAKING THE SASHES, BLOCKS, AND SETTING SQUARES

**1** Make the Flying Geese 1's using light A's and dark C's. Make the Flying Geese 2's with gold A's and purple print C's. Align an A on C, right sides together. Sew from corner to corner and trim the seam allowances to ¼″. Open the A patch and press. Repeat with another A on the other side. Using these units, piece the sashes.

Stitch & Flip

Stitch & Flip

Flying Geese 1's

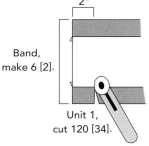

Flying Geese 1,
make 560 [176].

Flying Geese 2,
make 144 [48].

Sash,
make 140 [44].

**2** Referring to the strip-piecing diagram, make the bands and cut them into the Unit 1's.

**3** Using 5 dark and 4 light A's for each block, piece the blocks as shown. Noting the placement of the light and dark D's, make the Setting Square 1's and 2's.

2″

Band,
make 6 [2].

Unit 1,
cut 120 [34].

Unit 1

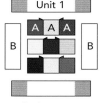

B          B

B

Block Piecing,
make 60 [17].

 D D D

Setting Square 1
Piecing,
make 45 [16].

Setting Square 2,
make 36 [12].

## MAKING THE SIDE AND CORNER UNITS

**1** To make a Side Unit, turn under the ¼″ seam allowances on 2 adjacent sides of a light purple A and blindstitch to the corner of E as shown. Make 16 [6] Side Units.

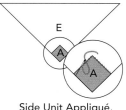

E

A

A

Side Unit Appliqué,
make 16 [6].

**2** To make a Corner Unit, first make a Unit 2. Turn under the ¼″ seam allowances of 3 edges of a Unit 2 as shown. Matching raw edges, center a Unit 2 on the long edge of an F patch and appliqué the 3 turned-under edges in place. Repeat to make 4 [4] Corner Units.

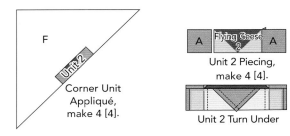

F

Unit 2

Corner Unit
Appliqué,
make 4 [4].

A  Flying Geese 2  A

Unit 2 Piecing,
make 4 [4].

Unit 2 Turn Under

## ASSEMBLING THE TOP

**1** Referring to the appropriate Assembly diagram, join sashes, blocks, and setting squares into rows, alternating sash orientations as shown. (Flying Geese 2's will join to setting square 2's.) Join row pairs and row groups. Join these to their side units. Sew these row units together. Join the corner units to the quilt.

**2** Matching centers, sew the border strips to the quilt. Miter the corners, trim the seam allowances to ¼″, and press open.

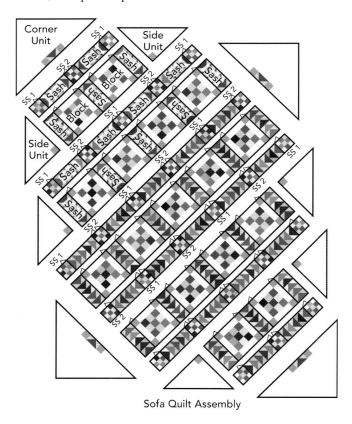

Sofa Quilt Assembly

# Quilting and Finishing

**1** To make a full-size pattern for the border 2 **Floral Cascade Quilting** motif (page 26), first fold tracing paper in half. Align the fold with the dotted line on the pattern and trace. Then flip the paper over and trace the other half. Repeat for the border corner motif.

**2** Referring to the Quilting Placement diagram, mark the motifs in the blocks and Flying Geese. Matching dots, mark repeats of the border corner motif shown in purple. Mark the leaf shown in red by tracing one from the corner motif. Center and mark the border motif in each side and corner unit.

**3** Layer the backing, batting, and quilt top and baste the layers together.

**4** Quilt the marked motifs in the blocks and Flying Geese. Using the patchwork as a guide, quilt the straight lines as shown. Quilt the marked motifs in the borders and units.

**5** Bind the quilt.

Quilting Placement

Arrows indicate direction for continuous-line machine quilting.

King Comforter Assembly

Floral Cascade
Quilting

½ Floral Cascade
Quilting

Arrows indicate direction for
continuous-line machine quilting.

Start

# Country
## roses

Designed and made by Turid Margaret Uren,
Bergen, Norway.

Turid made the traditional Drunkard's Path blocks for *Country Roses* while working on an offshore oil rig in the North Sea as a traffic controller for helicopters and vessels. She did not have a sewing machine, so she thought this was a fine opportunity to practice hand piecing. The flowers emerged after playing with the patches.

| QUILT SIZE: | | Topper |
|---|---|---|
| | | 67½″ × 83½″ |
| **FINISHED BLOCK:** | | |
| 16″ | | |
| **YARDAGE:** (44″ fabric) | | |
| **Cream Solid** | | 2⅜ yards |
| border 2 strips* | sides | 2 at 7½″ × 81″ |
| | top/bottom | 2 at 7½″ × 65″ |
| **Assorted Cream Prints** | | 2⅜ yards |
| | | 96 A, 96 B |
| **Red Solid**** | | 2 yards |
| border 1 strips*** | sides | 2 at 1¼″ × 66½″ |
| | top/bottom | 2 at 1¼″ × 52″ |
| **Navy Solid** | | 2⅝ yards |
| border 3 strips*** | sides | 2 at 3½″ × 86″ |
| | top/bottom | 2 at 3½″ × 70″ |
| **Teal Solid** | | ⅝ yard |
| double-fold binding | | 9 at 2¼″ × 38″ |
| **Green Solid** | | ¾ yard |
| bias strips | | 9 at 1½″ × 38″ |
| **Green Prints** | | ½ yard |
| | | 64 D |
| **Assorted Prints** | | 3 yards |
| | | 96 A, 96 B, 36 C, 36 D |
| **Backing** | | 5⅓ yards |
| panels | | 2 at 37″ × 88″ |
| **Batting** | | 72″ × 88″ |

\* An extra 3½″ has been added to the length and 1″ to the
width for insurance. After appliqué is complete, center and
trim each border 2 strip to 6½″ wide.

\*\* If you'd prefer to piece border 1, you will only need ¼ yard.
Cut 6 strips 1¼″ wide from selvage to selvage. Join them
and cut to required lengths.

\*\*\*An extra 2″ has been added to the length for insurance.

## ABOUT THIS QUILT

*For help with all phases of the quiltmaking process,
including appliqué mitered borders and blindstitching,
see Quilting Basics (pages 74–78).*

The assorted prints in this quilt are a variety of red,
green, navy, and purple small-scale floral prints in
medium and dark values. Their placement throughout
the quilt is random. For the cream prints, use a few
small-scale florals and include cream solid, too.

### TIP

When joining the A and B patches, sew with the convex
curve (patch A) on top. Pin the patches together at the
center of both curves and space additional pins about
1″ apart in both directions. While sewing, remove the pins
as you approach them.

## MAKING THE CENTER

1 Join the A and B patches
to make the blocks.

2 Sew the blocks together to
make the rows. Press the
seam allowances of every other
row in the same direction. Join
the rows and press these seam
allowances all the same way.

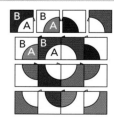

Block Piecing,
make 12.

Row,
make 4.

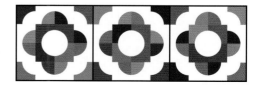

## Appliquéing the Border

1 To make an appliqué placement guide, transfer the bias stem, C's, D's, border 2 center line, and dotted lines given on pages 30–31 to tracing paper.

2 Fold each border 2 strip in half end-to-end and lightly press the center. Working out in both directions and in 8″ increments, lightly press creases as shown. Also crease the lengthwise center of each strip. Referring to the diagrams, match placement lines and creases and lightly trace the stem, reversing every other repeat.

3 Prepare the bias strips for appliqué, as described in Quilting Basics (page 76), *sewing ½″ from the fold.* Also prepare the appliqué with your preferred method. For each border 2 strip, first position and blindstitch the stem, stopping at the last crease at each end. Pin the stems away from the corners; the ends will be blindstitched in place after the borders are mitered in the next section.

4 Blindstitch the patches in alphabetical order. Press each border 2 strip right side down on a padded ironing board, avoiding the pins at each end. Centering the appliqué, trim each strip to 6½″ wide.

## Assembling the Top

1 Sew the border 1 side strips to the quilt; trim excess length. Repeat for the border 1 top and bottom strips.

2 Matching centers, join the corresponding border 2 and 3 strips. Press the seam allowances toward the border 3 strips. Matching centers with the centers of border 1, add the border 2–3 strips, being careful not to catch the bias stems in the corners. Press the seam allowances toward the quilt center.

3 Miter the corners, trim seam allowances to ¼″, and press these seam allowances open.

4 Complete the appliqué in each border 2 corner, adding the bias stems first and then the C's and D's. Press the corner appliqué right side down on a padded ironing board.

Top/Bottom Appliqué Border 2, make 2.

Side Appliqué Border 2, make 2.

Appliquéd
Border Corner

# QUILTING AND FINISHING

**1** Mark the **Rose Blossom Quilting** (page 30) in Patch A in the blocks. Mark the leaf motif in the border 3 strips, using the block seamlines for placement. Mark the corners as shown.

**2** Layer and baste together the backing, batting, and quilt top.

**3** Outline quilt the A and B patches. Outline quilt ⅛″ in from border 2 and around the appliqué. Quilt the marked motifs.

**4** Bind the quilt.

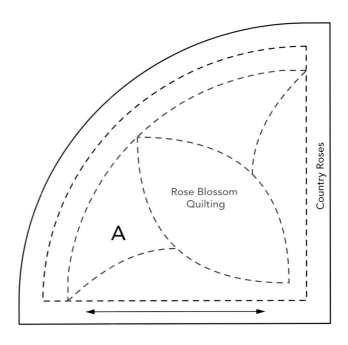

Rose Blossom Quilting

Country Roses

A

Quilting Placement

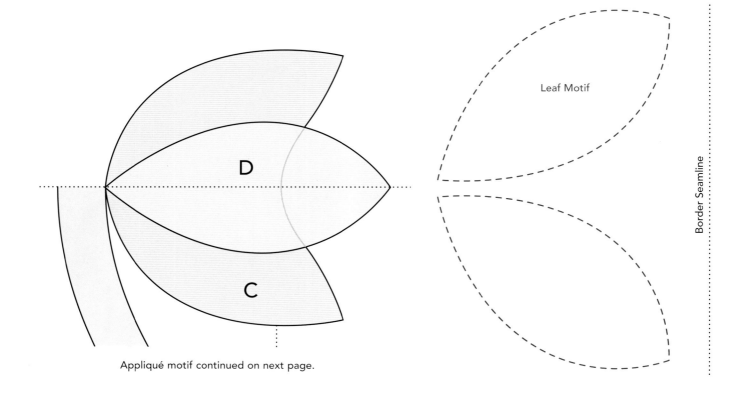

D

C

Leaf Motif

Border Seamline

Appliqué motif continued on next page.

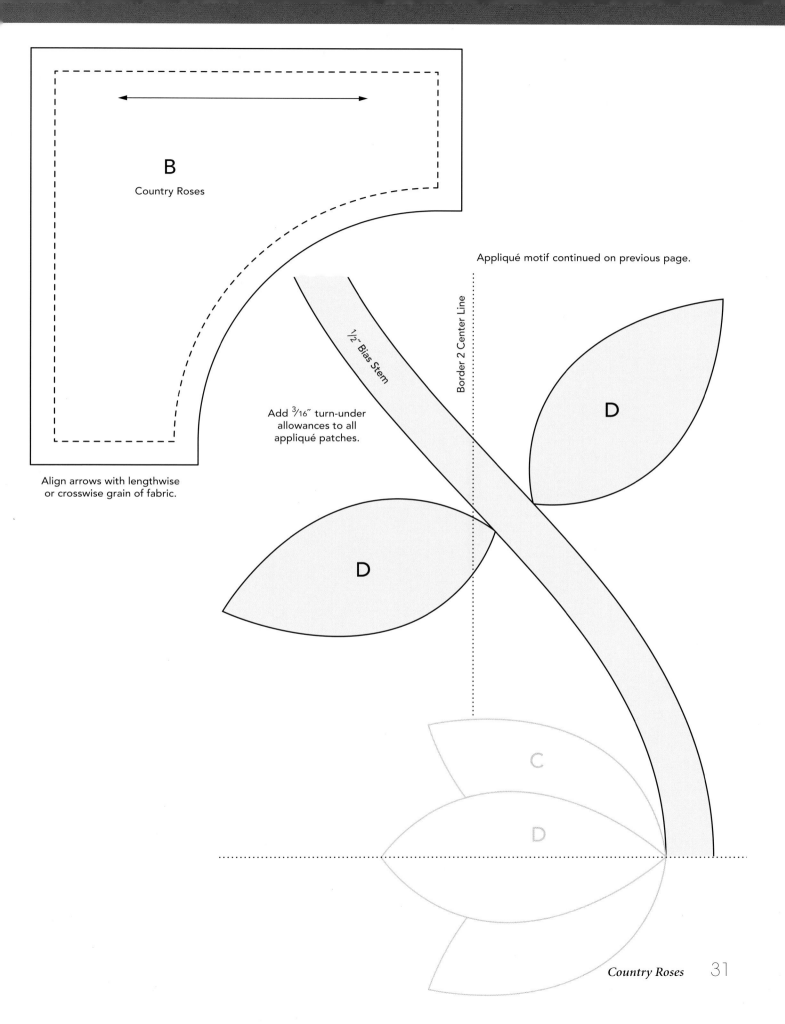

**B**

Country Roses

Align arrows with lengthwise
or crosswise grain of fabric.

½" Bias Stem

Add ³/₁₆" turn-under
allowances to all
appliqué patches.

Appliqué motif continued on previous page.

Border 2 Center Line

**D**

**D**

C

D

# Summer
## breeze

Designed by Marla Stefanelli. Made by Peg Spradlin. Fabrics from South Sea Imports and Chanteclaire Fabrics.

**W**hen we first published Summer Breeze in *Quiltmaker* March/April '94 (No. 36), we described it as a traditional favorite, and that has proven true with our readers. The Summer Breeze block is a variation of the traditional Summer Winds block.

**INTERMEDIATE**

## MATERIALS AND CUTTING

| QUILT SIZE: | Double Coverlet/Queen Comforter (shown) | Topper/Wall Quilt |
|---|---|---|
| | 86″ × 102″ | 54″ × 54″ |
| **BLOCK SIZE:** | | |
| 12″ | | |
| **YARDAGE:** (44″ fabric) | | |
| **Muslin** | 4¾ yards | 1¾ yards |
| | 182 B, 720 C, 120 D, 4 G | 68 B, 216 C, 36 D, 4 G |
| **Print Scraps** | 4⅝ yards | 1¾ yards |
| | 50 A, 120 B, 844 C | 13 A, 36 B, 280 C |
| **Yellow Print** | 3 yards | 1¾ yards |
| border 2 strips*    sides | 2 at 2½″ × 100½″ | 2 at 2½″ × 52½″ |
|    top/bottom | 2 at 2½″ × 88½″ | 2 at 2½″ × 56½″ |
| **Green Print** | 2¾ yards | 1½ yards |
| border 1 strips**    sides | 2 at 1½″ × 92½″ | 2 at 1½″ × 44½″ |
|    top/bottom | 2 at 1½″ × 82½″ | 2 at 1½″ × 50½″ |
| | 4 F | 4 F |
| **Red Print** | ⅞ yard | ⅝ yard |
| double-fold binding | 11 at 2¼″ × 37″ | 7 at 2¼″ × 35″ |
| **Pink Print** | 1⅞ yards | ⅝ yard |
| | 49 E | 12 E |
| **Backing** | 8 yards | 3½ yards |
| panels | 3 at 36″ × 90″ | 2 at 30″ × 58″ |
| sleeve | none for this size | 1 at 9″ × 54″ |
| **Batting** | 90″ × 106″ | 58″ × 58″ |

\* An extra 2″ has been added to the length for insurance.

\*\* Seam allowance is included in the length but no extra has been added for insurance.

## ABOUT THIS QUILT

*For help with all phases of the quiltmaking process, see Quilting Basics (pages 74–78).*

Directions are for both the double coverlet/queen comforter and the topper/wall quilt. Information that differs for the smaller size is given in brackets.

## BATTING TIPS

Before layering and basting your quilt sandwich, you will need to prepare the batting. For batting that requires prewashing, follow the manufacturer's instructions. If your batting does not require prewashing or if you wish to wash your quilt after it is finished for a puckered, antique look, unroll the batting and allow the wrinkles to relax overnight.

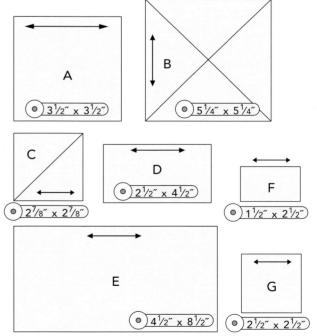

A
3½″ × 3½″

B
5¼″ × 5¼″

C
2⅞″ × 2⅞″

D
2½″ × 4½″

F
1½″ × 2½″

E
4½″ × 8½″

G
2½″ × 2½″

A corner-trimming template and directions for using it are in Quilting Basics.

## MAKING THE BLOCKS AND UNITS

1 Before you start piecing the blocks, sashes, and units, prepare your fabrics as described in *A Light Starch* (page 35). To better acquaint you with the block piecing, we recommend that you first make a test block. Use this block for the label if you like.

2 Following the piecing diagrams, make the blocks, sashes, and border units. Press the seam allowances as shown.

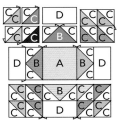 

Block Piecing, make 30 [9].

Sash Piecing, make 49 [12].

Border Unit, make 84 [44].

### TIP

Half-square triangle paper foundations, like *Thangles* or *Triangles on a Roll*, make piecing the C's easy and accurate. Look for paper foundations that finish at 2″ at your favorite quilt shop.

## ASSEMBLING AND JOINING THE ROWS

1 Join the blocks and sashes to make the Row 1's. Press the seam allowances toward the sashes.

2 To make the Row 2's, sew the A's and sashes together, again pressing the seam allowances toward the sashes.

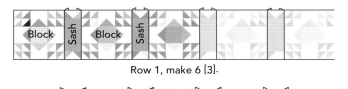

Row 1, make 6 [3].

Row 2, make 5 [2].

Topper/wall quilt is shown in darker colors.
Double coverlet/queen comforter includes the complete diagram.

3 Start with a Row 1 and alternate types to join the rows. Press the seam allowances toward the Row 2's.

## MAKING THE PIECED BORDER

1 To piece a side strip for border 1, join 23 [11] border units. Then add a corresponding green print strip. Make 2 [2].

2 For each top and bottom border 1 strip, join 19 [11] border units. To the ends of these strips, sew the F and G patches. Add the green print strips.

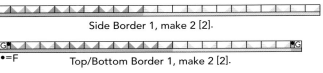

Side Border 1, make 2 [2].

Top/Bottom Border 1, make 2 [2].

•=F

## ADDING THE BORDERS

Join the border 1 side strips to the quilt and then add the top and bottom strips. Now sew the side border 2 strips to the quilt and trim the excess length. Press the seam allowances toward these strips. Repeat for the top and bottom strips.

## QUILTING AND FINISHING

**1** See *Batting Tips* (page 33), for hints on preparing your batting. If you wish to re-create the "period feel," use 100% cotton batting. Stretch the backing taut with the wrong side facing up. Layer the batting and quilt top on the backing. Baste the layers together.

**2** Using the patchwork as your guide, quilt a diagonal grid across the quilt as shown.

Quilting Placement

**3** Bind the quilt.

**4** To display the wall quilt, sew a sleeve to the backing.

## A LIGHT STARCH

Starching fabric before you cut patches will greatly improve your machine-piecing accuracy. Bias edges won't stretch, patches will keep their shape, and fabric won't be pulled into the machine needle hole. Starching also makes cutting and marking easier and more accurate because fabric won't bubble in front of the rotary cutter or marker. And because starch acts as a stain guard, marked lines are easier to remove.

We prefer a liquid starch-and-water solution instead of spray starch, because the solution penetrates your fabric to stabilize it while spray only coats it (and your iron and ironing surface). After washing, dunk the wet fabric in a 50/50 solution of liquid starch and water. Two cups of solution will starch 3 yards of fabric. Let the fabric soak and then squeeze out the excess. Store any leftover starch mixture in the refrigerator to prevent the solution from mildewing. Hang to damp dry and steam press on a cotton setting from the wrong side to remove any wrinkles. If the fabric has already dried, lightly mist with water and then iron. Your fabric should be as stiff as notebook paper.

Store your starched fabric flat (under the bed!) or roll it on leftover cardboard wrapping-paper tubes.

When you pin baste the quilt layers together, you may find that you need a little more muscle to push the pins through the layers. Quilting by machine is preferred for a starched quilt top; it's a bit difficult to pass a hand-quilting needle through the fabric. Starching the backing will also help eliminate tucks. Rinse your quilt after it is completed to remove the starch. Then stand back and enjoy all those perfect points!

# Too many geese

**Designed and made by Linda Foster,
Lee's Summit, Missouri.
Quilted by Rita Brenner.**

Linda bought the cabbage rose floral print without knowing what to make with it. One day, she saw a flock of geese in a parking lot and suddenly knew that Goose Tracks blocks were the perfect thing for fall colors. A border of Flying Geese seemed a natural finish.

MATERIALS AND CUTTING

| QUILT SIZE: | Sofa Quilt (shown) | Long Twin Comforter |
|---|---|---|
| | 57" × 72" | 72" × 99" |
| **BLOCK SIZE:** | | |
| 14" | | |
| **YARDAGE:** (44" fabric) | | |
| **Cream Print** | 1 yard | 1¾ yards |
| | 96 B, 48 C, 48 E | 192 B, 96 C, 96 E |
| **Tan Scraps** | 1⅔ yards | 2⅓ yards |
| | 96 B, 140 H | 192 B, 196 H |
| **Red Prints** | 3 at ⅜ yard | 4 at ½ yard |
| from each | 16 D, 8 G | 24 D, 10 G |
| **Red Scraps** | ⅛ yard | none for this size |
| | 4 G | |
| **Teal Print** | 1⅔ yards | 2¼ yards |
| double-fold binding | 8 at 2¼" × 37" | 10 at 2¼" × 38" |
| | 24 F, 8 G, 16 H | 48 F, 10 G, 16 H |
| **Green Scraps** | ⅝ yard | ¾ yard |
| | 26 G | 38 G |
| **Black Print** | 1¾ yards | 2½ yards |
| inner border*          sides | 2 at 2" × 56½" | 2 at 2½" × 84½" |
|                         top/bottom | 2 at 2½" × 45½" | 2 at 2" × 60½" |
| | 12 A | 24 A |
| **Multiprint** | 1⅛ yards | 1⅔ yards |
| | 24 F, 8 G, 4 I | 48 F, 10 G, 4 I |
| **Backing** | 3⅝ yards | 6¼ yards |
| panels | 2 at 39" × 61" | 2 at 39" × 103" |
| **Batting** | 61" × 76" | 76" × 103" |

*Seam allowance is included in the length but no extra has been added for insurance.
Border widths vary so that the outer pieced border of Flying Geese can fit perfectly.

## ABOUT THIS QUILT

*For help with all phases of the quiltmaking process, see Quilting Basics (pages 74–78).*

Directions are for both the sofa quilt and the long twin comforter. Information specific to the long twin size is given in brackets.

This quilt shows the success of picking a multicolored print first and coordinating other fabrics with it. Dark reds, teal, tans, and greens all echo the coloring of the large floral print of the blocks. See *Bias Alert* (page 38) for how to keep the bias edges of triangles from stretching.

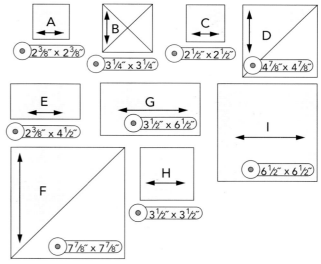

Align arrows with lengthwise or crosswise grain of fabric.
A corner-trimming template and directions for using it are in Quilting Basics.

## Making the Center

**1** Join the patches and press seam allowances as shown in the block piecing diagram. Make 12 [24] blocks.

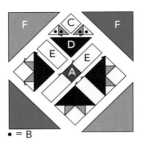

Block Piecing,
make 12 [24].

**2** Sew the blocks into rows. Press the seam allowances of every other row in the same direction. Sew the rows together, pressing seam allowances of all rows in the same direction.

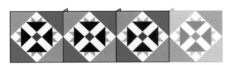

Row,
make 4 [6].

Sofa quilt is shown in darker colors.
Long twin comforter includes the complete diagram.

## Bias Alert

The bias edges of triangle patches,
such as the B's, D's, and F's, are naturally stretchy. To
stabilize them and prevent distortion while sewing,
lightly spritz the yardage with spray starch and press
before cutting.

## Adding the Borders

**1** Fold the inner border strips in half end-to-end and crease lightly. Matching centers and ends, sew the side strips to the quilt, easing in fullness if necessary. Press the seam allowances toward the strips. Add the top and bottom strips in the same way.

**2** To make the stitch-and-flip units, align H's on the corners of G's and I's as shown. Sew from corner to corner and trim seam allowances to ¼". Flip open the H's and press seam allowances toward the H's. Make 70 [98] Flying Geese units and 4 [4] Corner Units for the outer border.

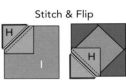

Flying Geese Unit,
make 70 [98].

Corner Unit,
make 4 [4].

**3** Join 20 [29] Flying Geese to make a strip for each side border and 15 [20] Flying Geese into a strip for the top and bottom borders. Add a corner unit to each end of the top and bottom border strips. Press seam allowances toward the corner units.

Side Border,
make 2 [2].

Top/Bottom Border,
make 2 [2].

Sofa quilt is shown in darker colors.
Long twin comforter includes the complete diagram.

**4** Matching centers and ends, add the side pieced border strips. Press seam allowances toward the inner border. Repeat for the top and bottom border strips.

# QUILTING AND FINISHING

**1** Layer and baste together the backing, batting, and top.

**2** **For hand quilting:** Make a template of the B/B/D patchwork and mark the **Goose Tracks Quilting** in the F Patches as shown below.

Outline quilt the border and all the patches except the B's and F's, then quilt the marked motifs.

Hand Quilting Placement

**3** **For machine quilting:** Meander quilt randomly over the surface.

**4** Bind the quilt.

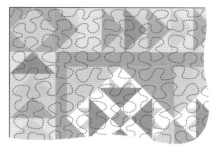

Machine Quilting Placement

# Pinwheel
## path

Designed by Peggy McCutcheon,
Etna, California.
Made by Penny Wolf.
Quilted by Faun Lee.
Fabrics from P&B Textiles.

This design reminded Peggy of streets and blocks, with the pinwheels representing activity. *Pinwheel Path* is good for showing off your quilting or a pretty fabric.

**MATERIALS AND CUTTING** · **INTERMEDIATE**

| QUILT SIZE: | | Sofa Quilt (shown) | Wide Queen Comforter |
|---|---|---|---|
| | | 54″ × 72″ | 92″ × 92″ |
| **BLOCK SIZE:** | | | |
| 9″ | | | |
| **YARDAGE:** (44″ fabric) | | | |
| **Large Multiprint** | | 1⅝ yards | 3⅜ yards |
| | | 288 A, 17 D | 656 A, 40 D |
| **Yellow Print** | | 1⅛ yards | 2⅛ yards |
| | | 284 A, 72 B | 652 A, 164 B |
| **Pink Print** | | 2 yards | 2⅝ yards |
| inner border* | sides | 2 at 2″ × 65½″ | 2 at 2″ × 83½″ |
| | top/bottom | 2 at 2″ × 50½″ | 2 at 2″ × 86½″ |
| | | 72 A | 164 A |
| **Blue Print** | | 1⅝ yards | 3½ yards |
| | | 144 A, 72 B, 68 E | 328 A, 164 B, 160 E |
| **Blue Plaid** | | 2⅛ yards | 2⅞ yards |
| outer border* | sides | 2 at 3½″ × 68½″ | 2 at 4½″ × 86½″ |
| | top/bottom | 2 at 3½″ × 56½″ | 2 at 4½″ × 94½″ |
| | | 144 C | 328 C |
| **Dark Blue Solid** | | ⅝ yard | ⅞ yard |
| double-fold binding | | 8 at 2¼″ × 36″ | 11 at 2¼″ × 37″ |
| **Backing** | | 3½ yards | 8¼ yards |
| panels | | 2 at 39″ × 58″ | 3 at 33″ × 96″ |
| **Batting** | | 58″ × 76″ | 96″ × 96″ |

\* An extra 2″ has been added to the length for insurance.

## ABOUT THIS QUILT

*For help with all phases of the quiltmaking process, see Quilting Basics (pages 74–78).*

Directions are for both the sofa quilt and the wide queen comforter. Information that differs for the larger size is given in brackets.

We have provided a quilting motif for the D Patch. However, if you choose a large-scale print for the D's, like we did, just use the print for a ready-to-quilt motif. Whether you are quilting by hand or by machine, consider choosing a fabric appropriate for this kind of quilting.

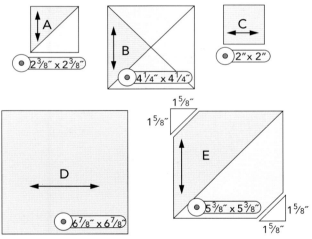

Align arrows with lengthwise or crosswise grain of fabric. A corner-trimming template and directions for using it are in Quilting Basics.

## Making the Blocks

Beginning with Block Y, construct the pinwheel, pressing open the allowance of the last seam sewn to reduce bulk in the center. Referring to the block piecing diagrams for patch placement and orientation, assemble the Y and Z blocks.

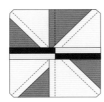

Pinwheel Pressing

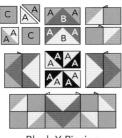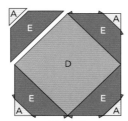

Block Y Piecing, make 18 [41].

Block Z, make 17 [40].

### Tip

When machine sewing along bias edges, use low speed. This reduces the possiblility of stretching the bias edges.

## Assembling the Top

1 Make the Row 1's and the Row 2's. Press the seam allowances of the Row 1's in one direction and those of the Row 2's in the opposite direction. Alternating types, join the rows.

2 Attach the inner side border strips, trim excess length, and press seam allowances toward the strips. Join the top and bottom border strips, trimming and pressing as before. Sew the outer border strips to the quilt in the same way.

Row 1, make 4 [5].

Row 2, make 3 [4].
Sofa quilt is shown in darker colors.
Wide queen comforter includes the complete diagram.

## Quilting and Finishing

1 If your fabric permits, quilt the D Patch by using the printed motifs as your guide. Quilting this way enhances the fabric design by defining the outline of the motif. If your fabric doesn't have a large-scale motif or if you prefer, trace the **Pinwheel Posey Quilting** (page 43) and transfer the complete motif to the D's and the partial purple motif to the E's as shown.

2 With the backing wrong side up, layer the batting and quilt top, and then baste with pins or thread.

3 Using the appropriate Quilting Placement guide, quilt the patches in the ditch. Quilt around fabric or marked motifs, and stipple quilt around the pinwheels as shown. Quilt the borders in the ditch. For the outer border, quilt a straight line through the center of the border.

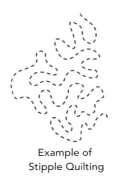

Example of Stipple Quilting

4 Bind the quilt.

Quilting Placement

Quilting Placement

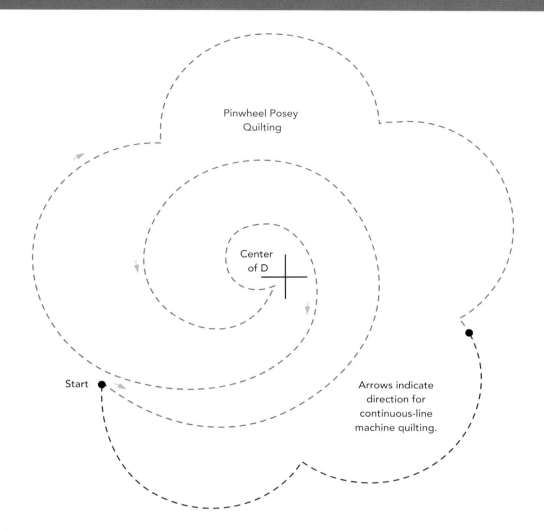

Pinwheel Posey
Quilting

Center
of D

Start

Arrows indicate
direction for
continuous-line
machine quilting.

# Patriotic
## seven sisters

Owned and quilted by Jeananne Wright,
Longmont, Colorado.

Jeananne believes this quilt top, which she purchased in Minnesota, was made for the state's centennial celebration in 1958. It was partially quilted, but she removed those stitches and quilted it herself.

| QUILT SIZE: | Wide Twin Comforter (shown) | Sofa Quilt |
|---|---|---|
| | 74″ × 88¾″ | 57″ × 71¾″ |
| **YARDAGE:** (44″ fabric) | | |
| **Red Solid** | ⅝ yard | ½ yard |
| | 120 A | 72 A |
| **White Solid** | 3¼ yards | 2¼ yards |
| double-fold binding | 9 at 2¼″ × 40″ | 8 at 2¼″ × 37″ |
| | 360 A, 120 B | 216 A, 72 B |
| **Blue Print** | 6¾ yards | 3⅞ yards |
| border strips*  sides | 2 at 3½″ × 85¼″ | 2 at 3½″ × 68¼″ |
| top/bottom | 2 at 3½″ × 76½″ | 2 at 3½″ × 59½″ |
| sashes* | 4 at 2¾″ × 70½″ | 3 at 2¾″ × 53½″ |
| | 720 A, 10 C, 10 Cr, 30 D | 432 A, 8 C, 8 Cr, 16 D |
| **Lining** | 5½ yards | 3⅝ yards |
| panels | 2 at 40″ × 93″ | 2 at 39″ × 61″ |
| **Batting** | 78″ × 93″ | 61″ × 76″ |

\* An extra 2″ has been added to the length for insurance.

## ABOUT THIS QUILT

*For help with all phases of the quiltmaking process, including making templates and sewing set-in patches, see Quilting Basics (pages 74–78).*

Directions are for both the wide twin comforter and the sofa quilt. Information specific to the sofa quilt is given in brackets.

If you compare the quilt in the photograph with our directions, you'll realize that this pattern approaches the construction of the quilt a bit differently. We have changed some setting patches to sashes to provide an easier way to sew the quilt. And, to make it fit today's bed sizes, the patterned quilt has wider borders.

## MAKING THE BLOCKS

To make a block, refer to the diagram below, join red A patches and blue A patches to make stars. Set in white A's around the red star; then add the blue stars and set in the remaining patches. Repeat to make 20 [12] blocks.

### TIP

For set-in patches, stop and start stitching at the seamlines. Don't sew into any seam allowances.

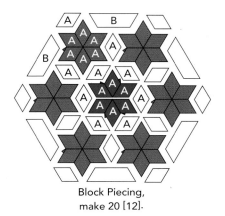

Block Piecing,
make 20 [12].

# ASSEMBLING THE TOP

**1** Join the blocks and the C, Cr, and D patches to make the rows. Press the rows well and measure the length of each row through its center. Using the measurement of the shortest row, cut the sashes to this length.

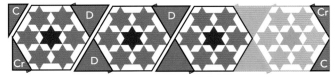

Row, make 5 [4].
Sofa quilt is shown in darker colors.
Wide twin comforter includes the complete diagram.

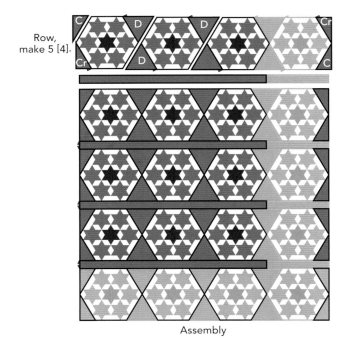

Row, make 5 [4].

Assembly

**2** Matching centers and ends and easing to fit as necessary, sew the sashes and rows together. Press these seam allowances toward the sashes.

**3** Sew the border side strips to the quilt. After pressing, trim any extra length. Add the top and bottom border strips in the same way.

# QUILTING AND FINISHING

**1** In the C, Cr, and D patches (page 47), mark lines 1″ apart, extending them into the sashes as shown.

**2** Layer the backing, batting, and the quilt top and baste the layers together.

**3** Outline quilt the A and B patches and then quilt as marked. Outline quilt the portions of sashes between the blocks. Finally, quilt lines ¼″ apart in the border.

**4** Bind the quilt.

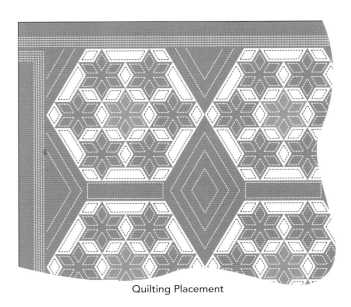

Quilting Placement

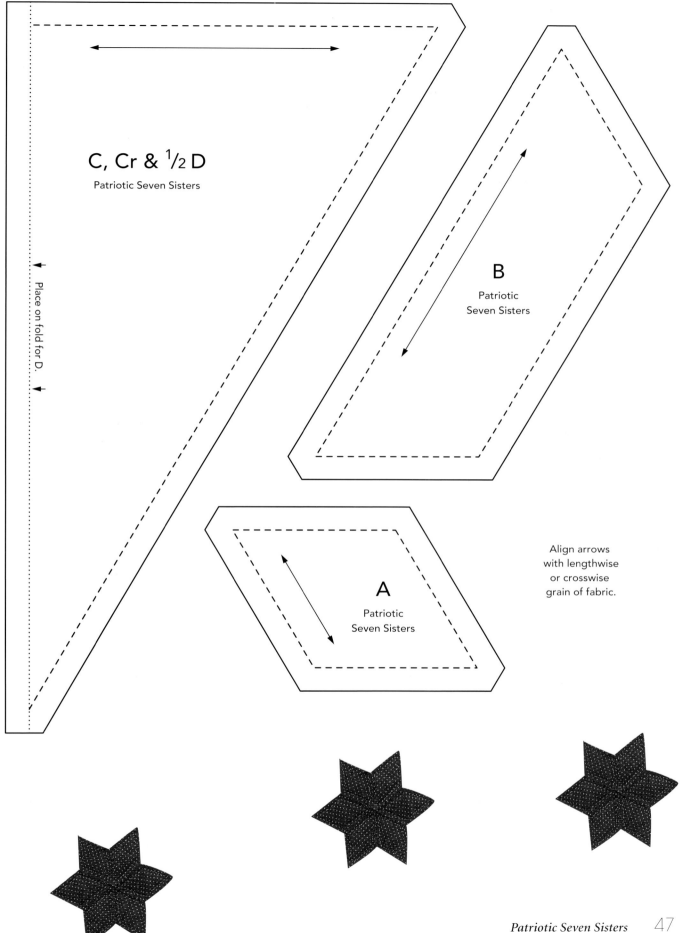

# C, Cr & ¹⁄₂ D

Patriotic Seven Sisters

Place on fold for D.

**B**

Patriotic
Seven Sisters

**A**

Patriotic
Seven Sisters

Align arrows
with lengthwise
or crosswise
grain of fabric.

# Appalachian
## trail

Designed and made by Patricia Gabriel, Conover, North Carolina.

Surprise someone special with this lovely, sure-to-be-an-heirloom quilt. Combine appliqué and three-dimensional embellishments to create charming bouquets—no two are exactly alike. *Appalachian Trail* graced the cover of the July/August '96 (No. 50) issue of *Quiltmaker* and has continued to be a favorite among our readers.

CHALLENGING

MATERIALS AND CUTTING

| QUILT SIZE: | Double Comforter (shown) | Queen Comforter |
|---|---|---|
| | 80¾" × 80¾" | 88¼" × 95¾" |
| **BLOCK SIZE:** | | |
| 7½" | | |
| **YARDAGE:** (44" fabric) | | |
| **Cream Print Scraps** | 5¾ yards | 7 yards |
| | 164 A, 160 B, 76 D, 4 E | 220 A, 220 B, 88 D, 4 E |
| **Pastel Print Scraps** | 4¼ yards | 6 yards |
| | 160 A, 164 B, yo-yos | 220 A, 220 B, yo-yos |
| **Pastel Solid Scraps** | 1⅛ yards | 1½ yards |
| for appliqué | flowers and folded hexagons | flowers and folded hexagons |
| **Blue Print Scraps** | 2⅜ yards | 2¾ yards |
| | 80 C | 92 C |
| **Blue Print** | 1⅔ yards | 1¾ yards |
| bias binding | 7 at 1⅛" × 51" | 8 at 1⅛" × 51" |
| **Green Solid Scraps** | ⅝ yard | ⅞ yard |
| for appliqué | leaves | leaves |
| **Green Print** | ⅓ yard | ½ yard |
| strips* | 8 at 1⅛" × 40" | 9 at 1⅛" × 40" |
| **Backing** | 7⅝ yards | 8⅓ yards |
| panels | 3 at 29" × 85" | 3 at 34" × 93" |
| **Batting** | 85" × 85" | 93" × 100" |

**SUPPLIES:** embroidery floss

\* To make the inner border strips, join 8 [9] strips end-to-end to make one strip. Cut this strip into two lengths 69¼" [84¼"] for the sides and two lengths 69¼" [76¾"] for the top and bottom. Seam allowance is included in the length but no extra has been added for insurance.

## ABOUT THIS QUILT

*For help with all phases of the quiltmaking process, including mitered borders and blindstitching, see Quilting Basics (pages 74-78).*

Directions are for both the double comforter and the queen comforter. Information that differs for the larger size is given in brackets.

If you want your quilt to look like the one shown, choose reproduction 1930s pastel prints (blues for the pieced border) and cream-on-cream prints. The colors gradiate in value from light in the center to medium at the edges of the quilt. The flower and leaf appliqués are mostly pastel solids, accented with print yo-yos and solid-color folded hexagons.

## MAKING AND JOINING THE BLOCKS

**1** Follow the block piecing diagrams to make the Y and Z blocks. Set the Z's aside.

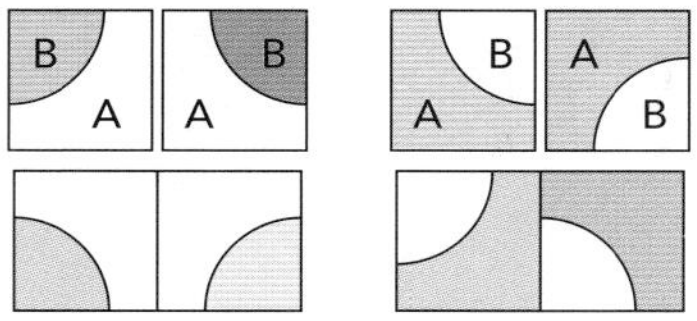

Block Y Piecing, make 41 [55].  Block Z Piecing, make 40 [55].

**2** See *Yo-Yos and Folded Hexagons* (page 51) to make these appliqué embellishments. Prepare a variety of appliqué patches, including yo-yos and folded hexagons, for each Y block.

**3** Combine appliqué patches (page 53) to create a different bouquet for each block. Pin or baste and then blindstitch the patches in place. With green floss, outline stitch a vein in each leaf and add the flower stems. Embellish some bouquets with French knots.

**4** Alternating types, arrange the Y and Z blocks in rows for a pleasing mix of color and floral designs. Join the blocks to make the Row 1's and Row 2's. Join the rows.

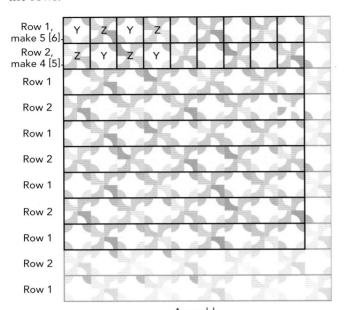

**Assembly**
Double comforter is shown in darker colors.
Queen comforter includes the complete diagram.

## MAKING THE PIECED BORDER

**1** Following the diagrams, join 20 [24] C's and 19 [23] D's to make 4 [2] pieced side border strips. [To make the pieced top and bottom border strips for the queen size, join 22 C's and 21 D's.] Press the seam allowances toward the C's.

Side Border, make 4 [2].

Top/Bottom Border, make 0 [2].

**2** Using template D (page 52) or its reverse as a guide, mark the placement dot on the D patches at the ends of each border strip, ⅞″ in from the end C/D seam.

## ADDING THE BORDERS

**1** Matching the centers and ends, pin an inner border strip to one side of the quilt. Beginning and ending stitches ¼″ from the quilt edges, sew the strip to the quilt. Repeat, adding inner border strips to the opposite side and the top and bottom of the quilt.

**2** Miter the corners, trim the seam allowances to ¼″, and press open. Mark a dot on each mitered border seam ¼″ in from both edges.

**3** Matching the dots on the inner border to the placement dots on the D's, pin a pieced border strip to its corresponding side. Easing any fullness, join each pieced border strip to the inner border *between the dots*. Miter the corners. Cut away excess C and D fabric to ¼″. Set in an E patch at each corner.

## QUILTING AND FINISHING

**1** Layer the backing, batting, and quilt top; baste. Quilt the blocks, the pastel B's, and the appliqué in the ditch. Outline quilt the curved edges of the pastel A's.

**2** In the border, outline quilt the patches. At the curved end of each C, quilt a second row of stitches ¼″ inside the first as shown.

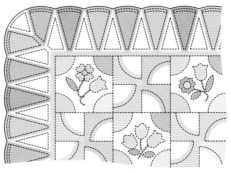

Quilting Placement

**3** Bind the quilt.

# YO-YOS AND FOLDED HEXAGONS

Yo-yos, gathered fabric circles, have been appliquéd on *Appalachian Trail*. Folded hexagons, also on the quilt, are a variation of the yo-yo design. We give circle patterns for making three different sizes of each. From each pattern you will get a yo-yo or a hexagon approximately one-half the diameter of the cut circle.

To make a folded hexagon, fold and finger press a circle in half horizontally and vertically. Beginning at a crease, fold the edge to the center. Next, fold in the outside right point (created by the first fold) to the center. Finger press the folds. Continue folding and finger pressing in this way until the hexagon is formed. Press the folds with your iron. Blindstitch the hexagon in place, covering the center with a tiny yo-yo.

To make a yo-yo, cut a circle and lay it right side down. Matching thread color to fabric, thread a needle and knot the ends together. Fold in the raw edge 1/8" as you sew around the circle with a medium-size running stitch, hiding the knot under the fold. Gather the circle closed, secure with a backstitch, and knot on the inside. Centering the gathered opening, blindstitch the yo-yo into place.

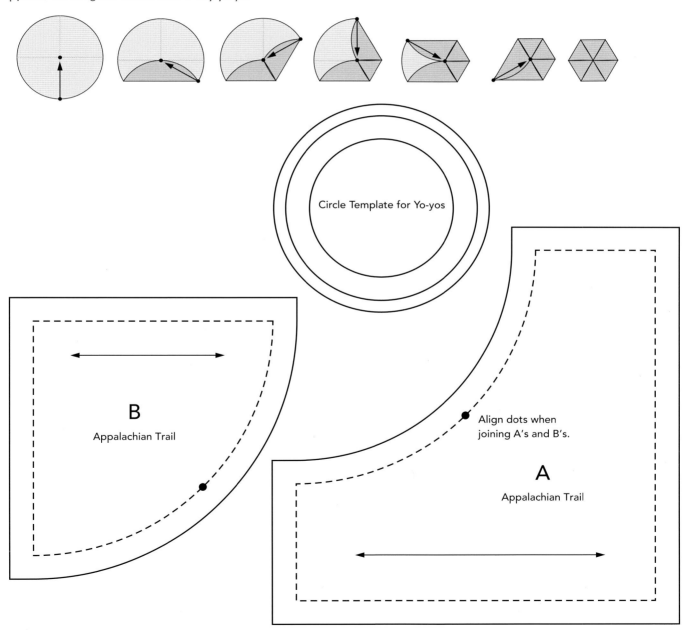

Circle Template for Yo-yos

B
Appalachian Trail

Align dots when joining A's and B's.

A
Appalachian Trail

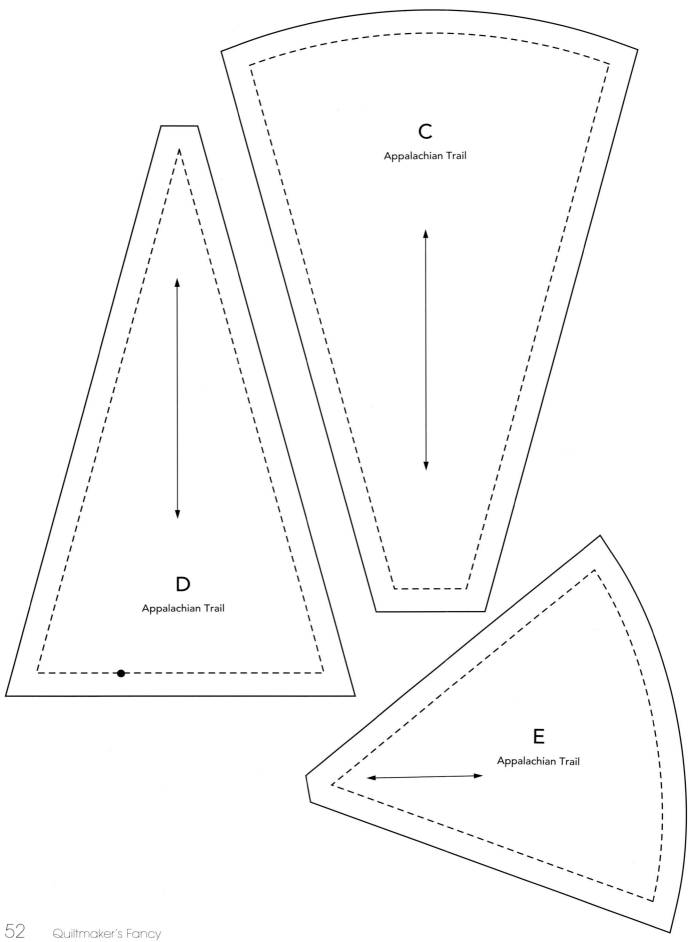

C

Appalachian Trail

D

Appalachian Trail

E

Appalachian Trail

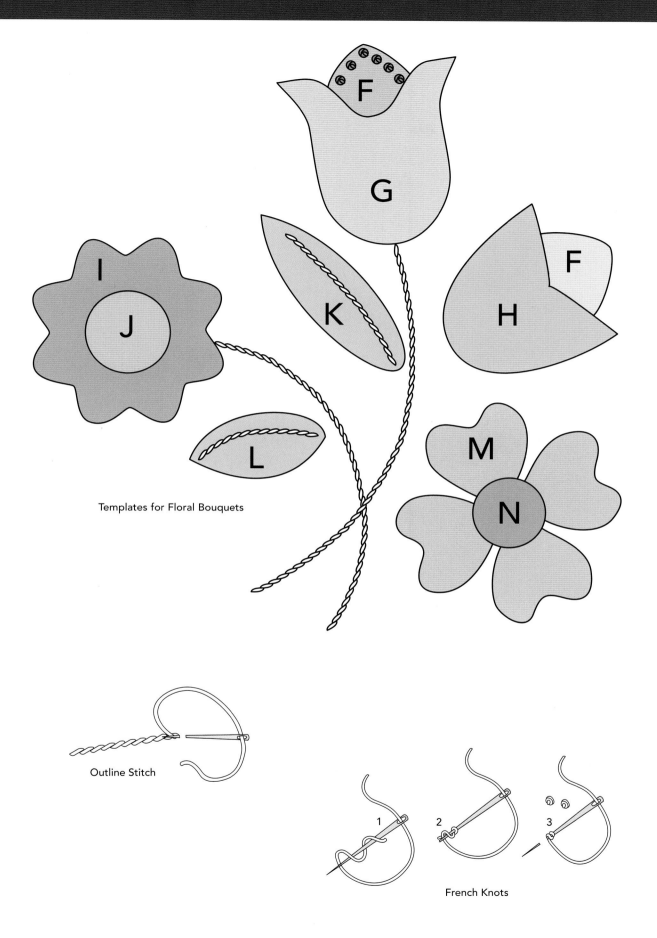

Templates for Floral Bouquets

Outline Stitch

French Knots

# Alpine summer

Designed by Annie Segal.
Made by Lucy Brown.

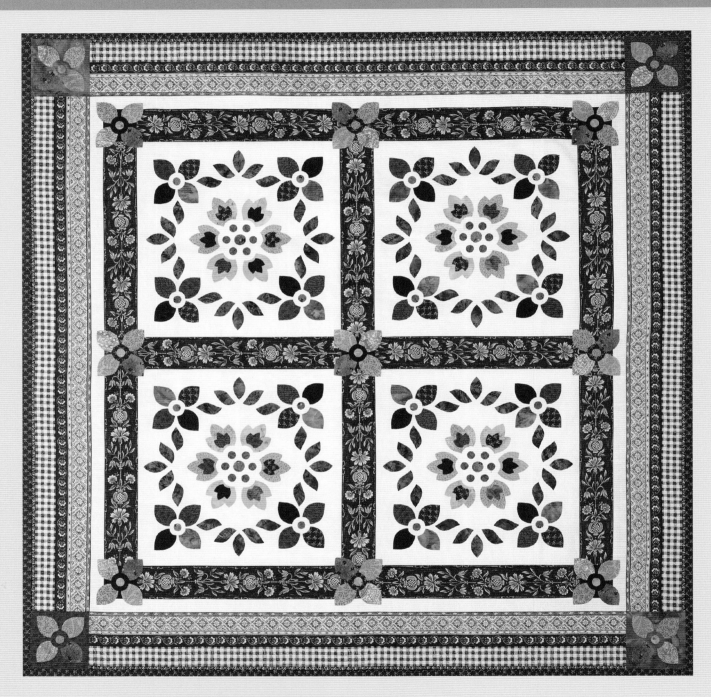

Although the wreath design has many patches, the finished block measures 15″ so you can construct the quilt top more quickly than you might think. The large block could also become a single-block wall quilt or the center of a medallion. Scrap reds and blues blend beautifully with the heavily patterned stripes. Should your stripe be more sedate, scraps will liven up the quilt.

MATERIALS AND CUTTING

| QUILT SIZE: | Wall Quilt (shown) | Twin Comforter |
|---|---|---|
| | 48½″ × 48½″ | 70″ × 87½″ |
| **BLOCK SIZE:** | | |
| 15″ | | |
| **QUILT REQUIRES:** | | |
| | 4 Y Blocks | 12 Y Blocks |
| | 4 Z Blocks | 4 Z Blocks |
| | (set 2 × 2) | (set 3 × 4) |
| **YARDAGE:** (44″ fabric) | | |
| **Red Print Scraps** | ⅝ yard | 1⅜ yards |
| | 24 E, 64 H, 9 I, 4 J | 72 E, 192 H, 20 I, 4 J |
| **Dark Red Print** | ½ yard | ⅝ yard |
| double-fold binding | 6 at 2¼″ × 37″ | 9 at 2¼″ × 38″ |
| **Yellow Solid** | 1⅜ yards | 4⅛ yards |
| inner border* sides | 2 at 1½″ × 40″ | 2 at 3½″ × 75″ |
| top/bottom | 2 at 1½″ × 42″ | 2 at 3½″ × 63½″ |
| | 4 A** | 12 A** |
| **Gold Print Scraps** | ¼ yard | ⅝ yard |
| | 13 C, 24 D | 24 C, 72 D |
| **Green Print** | 4″ × 10″ scrap | ⅛ yard |
| | 24 C | 72 C |
| **Teal Print** | ¼ yard | ¾ yard |
| | 32 F, 32 Fr, 16 G | 96 F, 96 Fr, 48 G |
| **Medium Blue Print Scraps** | ½ yard | ¾ yard |
| | 4 B, 16 C, 52 H | 12 B, 48 C, 96 H |
| **Multiprint Stripe*** | 2¾ yards | 7½ yards |
| outer border* sides | 2 at 5″ × 42″ | 2 at 5″ × 81″ |
| top/bottom | 2 at 5″ × 42″ | 2 at 5″ × 63½″ |
| sashes | 12 at 3″ × 15½″ | 31 at 3″ × 15½″ |
| **Nonstriped fabric** (for use in place of multiprint stripe above) | | |
| outer border* | 1⅜ yards | 2½ yards |
| sashes | ⅝ yard | 1½ yards |
| **Backing** | 3⅛ yards | 5½ yards |
| panels | 2 at 27″ × 53″ | 2 at 38″ × 92″ |
| sleeve | 1 at 9″ × 48″ | none for this size |
| **Batting** | 53″ × 53″ | 74″ × 92″ |

\* An extra 2″ has been added to the length for insurance.

\*\* Trim to 15½″ × 15½″ after appliqué is complete.

\*\*\*Adequate for a fabric that includes two different stripe motifs
with a minimum of two repeats per stripe across the width.

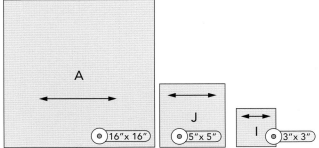

Align arrows with lengthwise or crosswise grain of fabric.

## ABOUT THIS QUILT

*For help with all phases of the quiltmaking process
including blindstitching, see Quilting Basics (pages 74–78).*

Directions are for both the wall quilt and the twin
comforter. Information that differs for the twin size is
given in brackets.

## COPYCAT CUTS

To see at a glance where to cut each border strip so they all match, tape a representative 1″ slice of the fabric to your acrylic ruler.

## CUTTING THE STRIPED FABRICS

Matching the placement of the stripe motif from sash to sash and from border strip to border strip makes a prettier quilt.

## MAKING THE BLOCKS

**1** Trace the full block appliqué (page 57), including the 2 center marks and the dotted lines. Fold all A, I, and J patches in half both ways to mark the centers, then unfold.

**2** For block Y, align the center and folds of A on the tracing. Mark the motif placement. Reposition 3 times to complete the motif. Repeat for all A's.

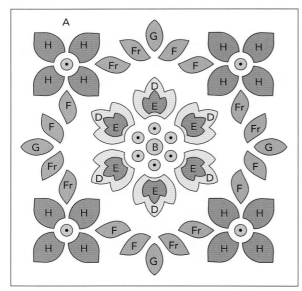

• = C                  Block Y, make 4 [12].

**3** For block Z, align the center of each J square on the tracing and transfer the design.

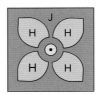

Block Z,
make 4 [4].
• = C

**4** For the I patches, align and mark the C and partial H's, which will be enough to use for placement.

**5** Prepare patches B–H (page 57) for appliqué using your favorite method. In alphabetical order, blindstitch the patches to the A's and J's to make the Y and Z blocks. Trim the Y blocks to 15½″ × 15½″. Set aside the remaining appliqué patches until after the quilt top is assembled.

## ASSEMBLING THE ROWS

**1** Make the sash and block rows as shown.

**2** Beginning with a sash row, join the block and sash rows, alternating types. Press all seam allowances between rows toward the sash rows.

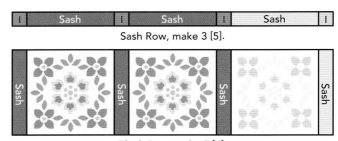

Sash Row, make 3 [5].

Block Row, make 2 [4].
Wall quilt is shown in darker colors.
Twin comforter includes the complete diagram.

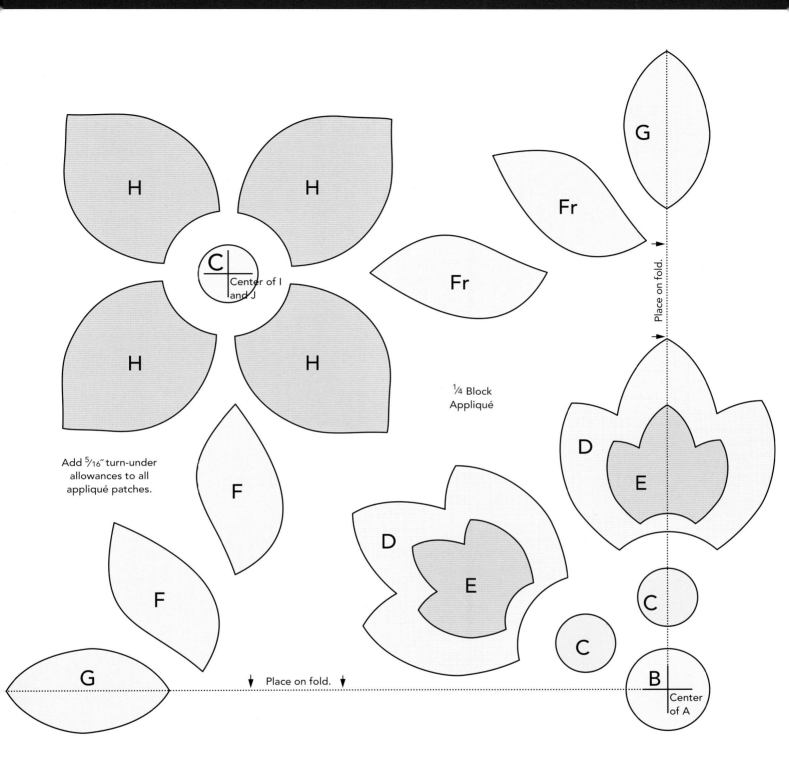

H

H

C
Center of I
and J

H

H

Fr

G

Fr

¼ Block
Appliqué

Place on fold.

Add ⁵⁄₁₆″ turn-under
allowances to all
appliqué patches.

F

D

E

D

E

C

F

C

G

Place on fold.

B
Center
of A

## ASSEMBLING THE TOP

1 Join the inner side border strips to the quilt, then the top and bottom strips, trimming lengths as needed. Blindstitch the appliqué patches to each I patch as shown.

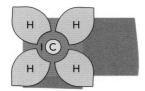

2 Measure the width of the quilt top through the middle from raw edge to raw edge. Trim the outer top and bottom border strips to this length. Join Z blocks to the ends of both strips.

3 Add the outer side border strips to the quilt, then the top and bottom pieced strips.

## QUILTING AND FINISHING

1 Starting in the center and working outward on each sash and border strip, mark the **Meadowsweet Quilting** as shown. By marking the motifs so they touch, you will be able to start at one end and machine quilt each "set" continuously.

2 Layer and baste the backing, batting, and the quilt top.

3 Quilt the A's, J's, sashes, and border strips in the ditch, stopping at the edges of appliqué patches that overlap the seams. Quilt the appliqué patches in the ditch and the motifs as marked.

Quilting Placement

4 Bind the quilt. Add a sleeve to the backing of the wall quilt.

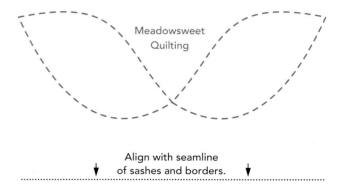

Meadowsweet Quilting

Align with seamline
of sashes and borders.

# Indiana
# feathered star

Designed and made by an unknown quiltmaker. Quilted by Jeananne Wright, Longmont, Colorado.

The "cheddar" color was frequently used as an accent in quilts from 1845–1885 but was not used in clothing. Known as *antimony* or *chrome orange*, this mineral dye became available as early as 1820 and was produced by heating chrome yellow in an alkaline solution. A good synthetic orange was not available until after World War I.

| QUILT SIZE: | | Queen Comforter (shown) | Sofa Quilt |
|---|---|---|---|
| | | 94″ × 94″ | 58½″ × 76¼″ |
| **FINISHED BLOCK:** | | | |
| 16″ | | | |
| **YARDAGE:** (44″ fabric) | | | |
| **Navy Print** | | 1 yard | ⅝ yard |
| | | 200 B | 96 B |
| **Red Print** | | 2⅞ yards | 2⅛ yards |
| border strips* | sides | 2 at 4″ × 89½″ | 2 at 4″ × 71¾″ |
| | top/bottom | 2 at 4″ × 96½″ | 2 at 4″ × 61″ |
| sashes** | | 4 at 2¼″ × 87½″ | 3 at 2¼″ × 52″ |
| | | 20 E | 8 E |
| **Orange Solid*** | | 2⅜ yards | 1⅛ yards |
| foundation patches | | 11, 12, 16, 20 | 11, 12, 16, 20 |
| **Brown Print Scraps*** | | 3 yards | 1½ yards |
| foundation patches | | 1, 3, 5, 6, 8, 10, 13, 15, 17, 19 | 1, 3, 5, 6, 8, 10, 13, 15, 17, 19 |
| **White Solid** | | 4⅝ yards | 2⅜ yards |
| double-fold binding | | 11 at 2¼″ × 38″ | 8 at 2¼″ × 38″ |
| | | 100 C, 100 D | 48 C, 48 D |
| **White Print** | | ¾ yard | ⅜ yard |
| | | 25 A | 12 A |
| **White Print Scraps *** | | 1⅞ yards | 1 yard |
| foundation patches | | 2, 4, 7, 9, 14, 18 | 2, 4, 7, 9, 14, 18 |
| **Backing** | | 8⅝ yards | 3¾ yards |
| panels | | 3 at 34″ × 98″ | 2 at 41″ × 63″ |
| **Batting** | | 98″ × 98″ | 63″ × 81″ |

\* An extra 2″ has been added to the length for insurance.

\*\* Seam allowance is included in the length but no extra has been added for insurance.

\*\*\*Although these yardages are adequate for foundation piecing, you may need more if you cut very generous patches.

## ABOUT THIS QUILT

*For help with all phases of the quiltmaking process, including foundation piecing and set-in patches, see Quilting Basics (pages 74–78).*

Directions are for both the queen comforter and the sofa quilt. Information specific to the sofa size is given in brackets.

Most of the blocks in this quilt are made from navy, orange, brown, and white fabrics. If you study the photograph, you'll see some variations on these colors and their placements in the blocks. For simplicity, this pattern is presented with fewer fabrics. If you have lots of scraps on hand, you might want to make your blocks scrappier, like the actual quilt. To make this quilt fit a queen-size bed, the yardage box lists borders cut wider than those on the photographed quilt. For help precutting oversized foundation patches, see *The Right Triangle* (page 61). To cut the A patches, use either the template or the rotary cutting diagram.

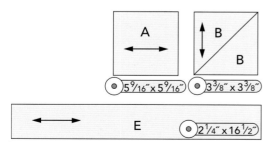

A    5⁹⁄₁₆″ x 5⁹⁄₁₆″
B    3⅜″ x 3⅜″
E    2¼″ x 16½″

Align arrows with lengthwise or crosswise grain of fabric. A corner-trimming template and directions for using it are in Quilting Basics.

## MAKING THE BLOCKS

**1** Using an accurate photocopier or by tracing, make 100 [48] copies each of Sections 1–4 (pages 62–63). Following numerical order, foundation piece the sections.

**2** Join the sections and the patches, setting in the D's last. Make 25 [12] blocks. Remove the foundation papers.

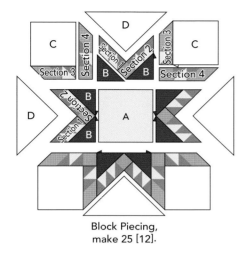

Block Piecing,
make 25 [12].

## ASSEMBLING THE TOP

**1** Join the blocks and the E patches to make the rows. Beginning with a row and alternating types, join the rows and the sashes.

Row, make 5 [4].
Sofa quilt is shown in darker colors.
Queen comforter includes the complete diagram.

**2** For the squared border, sew the side strips to the quilt and press the seam allowances toward the strips. Trim any extra length. Repeat to add the top and bottom strips.

## QUILTING AND FINISHING

**1** Trace a single **Petal Quilting** motif (page 63) on see-through template plastic and cut it out. Referring to the diagram and beginning at the border seamlines in each corner, mark the border, sashes, and E patches. Mark a 1¼″ grid in the A and D patches and a 1″ grid in the C's. Then mark diagonal lines through the grids.

## TIP

Instead of marking the grid, after the quilt is layered and basted, use masking tape as a guide. Remember to remove the tape after every quilting session.

**2** Layer and baste together the backing, batting, and quilt top.

**3** Outline quilt the patches as shown and then quilt as marked.

**4** Bind the quilt.

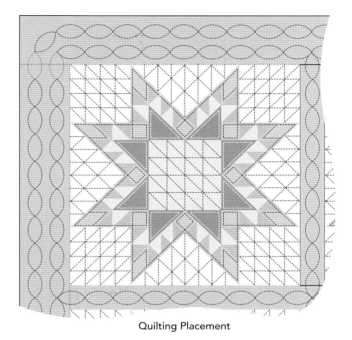

Quilting Placement

## THE RIGHT TRIANGLE

To conserve fabric and speed up the sewing process, precut the patches for foundation piecing. Cut the brown print and white print scraps into 2¾″ squares and then cut each square in half diagonally. The triangles are cut to the proper angle and are adequately sized to cover their foundation patches.

2¾″

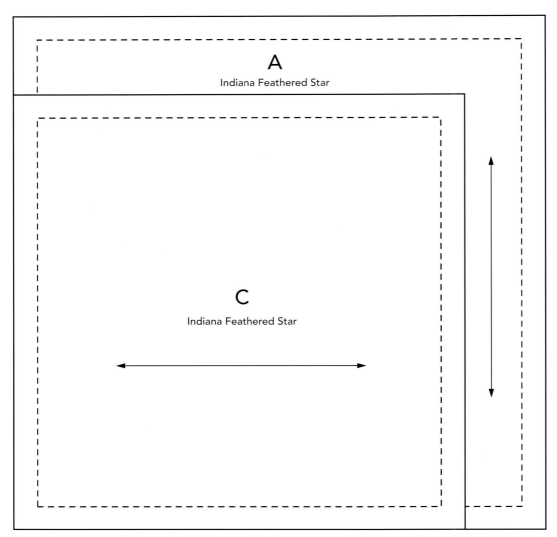

A
Indiana Feathered Star

C
Indiana Feathered Star

Align arrows with lengthwise or crosswise grain of fabric.

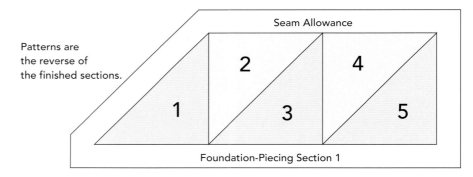

Seam Allowance

Patterns are
the reverse of
the finished sections.

2    4

1    3    5

Foundation-Piecing Section 1

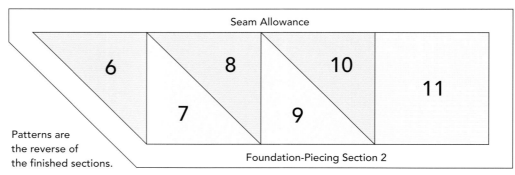

Seam Allowance

6    8    10

7    9    11

Patterns are
the reverse of
the finished sections.

Foundation-Piecing Section 2

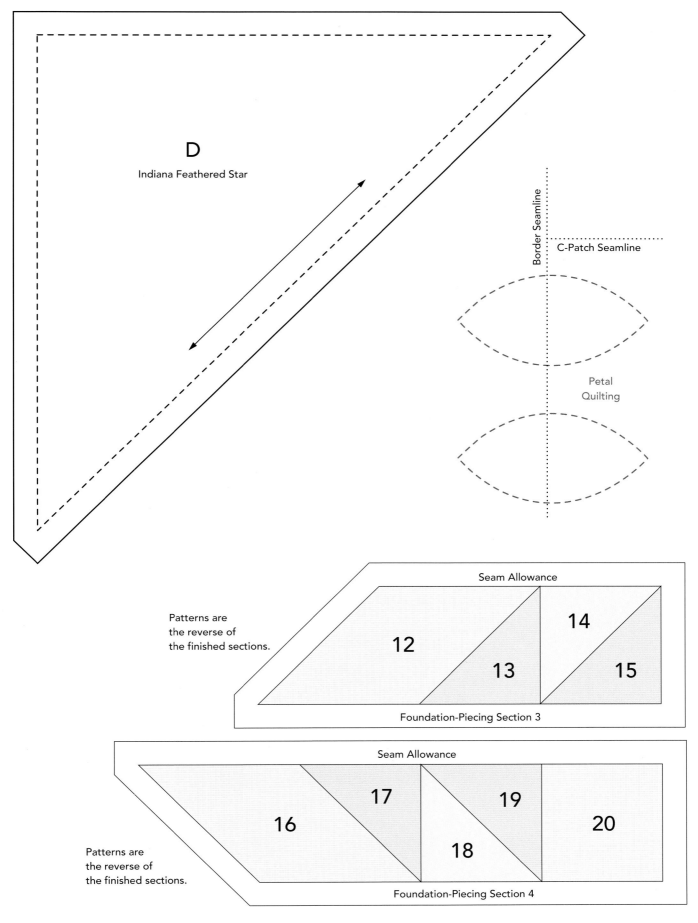

D

Indiana Feathered Star

Border Seamline

C-Patch Seamline

Petal
Quilting

Patterns are
the reverse of
the finished sections.

Seam Allowance

12

13

14

15

Foundation-Piecing Section 3

Patterns are
the reverse of
the finished sections.

Seam Allowance

16

17

18

19

20

Foundation-Piecing Section 4

# American rose

Designed by Barbara Baume,
Southington, Connecticut.
Made by Linda Holst.
Quilted by Maria Reardon Capp.

This quilt graced the cover of the July/August '94 (No. 38) issue of *Quiltmaker*. Its designer, Barbara Baume of Southington, Connecticut, combined classic appliqué with Log Cabin patchwork and pieced sashing—an innovative union for some of the traditional elements of quiltmaking.

**MATERIALS AND CUTTING**

CHALLENGING

| QUILT SIZE: | Wall Quilt/Topper (shown) | Long Double Comforter |
|---|---|---|
| | 53½" × 53½" | 76" × 98½" |
| **BLOCK SIZE:** | | |
| 20" | | |
| **YARDAGE:** (44" fabric) | | |
| **Tan Print** | 1⅓ yards | 3 yards |
| | 4 A, 4 F, 36 I, 192 R | 12 A, 12 F, 84 I, 494 R |
| **Gold Multiprint** | ¼ yard | ⅜ yard |
| | 16 H | 48 H |
| **Light Blue Print** | ½ yard | 1½ yards |
| | 16 B | 48 B |
| **Dark Blue Print** | 1¾ yards | 2⅞ yards |
| border strips* — sides | 2 at 3½" × 50" | 2 at 3½" × 95" |
| border strips* — top/bottom | 2 at 3½" × 56" | 2 at 3½" × 78½" |
| | 128 I | 384 I |
| **Rose Scraps**** | 1¼ yards | 3 yards |
| | 4 E, 16 G, 16 J, 16 K, 16 L, 16 M, 16 N, 16 O, 16 P | 12 E, 48 G, 48 J, 48 K, 48 L, 48 M, 48 N, 48 O, 48 P |
| **Red Print** | ⅔ yard | 1½ yards |
| | 4 D, 105 Q | 12 D, 268 Q |
| **Red/Black Print** | ⅝ yard | ¾ yard |
| double-fold binding | 7 at 2¼" × 34" | 10 at 2¼" × 37" |
| **Green Scraps**** | ½ yard | 1¼ yards |
| bias strips | 8 at 1" × 11" | 24 at 1" × 11" |
| straight-grain strips | 4 at 1" × 14" | 12 at 1" × 14" |
| | 128 C | 384 C |
| **Backing** | 3½ yards | 6⅛ yards |
| panels | 2 at 30" × 58" | 2 at 41" × 103" |
| sleeve | 1 at 9" × 53" | none for this size |
| **Batting** | 58" × 58" | 80" × 103" |

\* An extra 2" has been added to the length for insurance.

\*\* See the tip *The Value of Your Fabrics* (page 66) for help in choosing and cutting the scrap fabrics.

## ABOUT THIS QUILT

*For help with all phases of the quiltmaking process, including bias strips and blindstitching, see Quilting Basics (pages 74–78).*

Directions are for both the wall quilt/topper and double comforter. Information that differs for the double size is given in brackets.

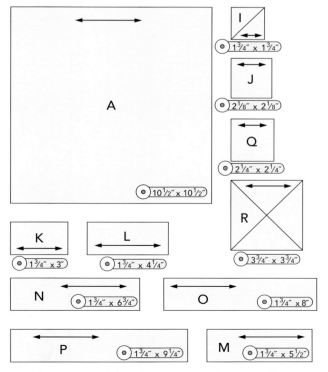

Align arrows with lengthwise or crosswise grain of fabric.

## The Value of Your Fabrics

Quilters value their fabric collections in dollars and cents, but there is another value to consider—color value. The lightness or darkness of a fabric, known as "value," plays an important role in a quilt's appearance, whether you work with a limited number of fabrics or a wide variety of scraps.

The medium-value J patch in the American Rose block is surrounded by light, medium, and then darker "logs." Separate your rose-colored scraps into light, medium, and dark values. Cut K's and L's from the lights; J's, M's, and N's from the mediums; and O's and P's from the darks.

The placement of scrap greens is more relaxed. The stems are dark in value, but the leaves are a random combination of both medium and dark.

For continuity from block to block, make all flowers the same, with the center a lighter value than the outer ring of petals. Cut all the green strips from the same scrap.

Although there is quite a mix of scraps in this quilt, it may be that American Rose catches your eye because of the thought that went into the placement of color values.

## Making the Blocks, Sashes, and Row 1's

Following the diagrams, piece the blocks, the sashes, and the Row 1's.

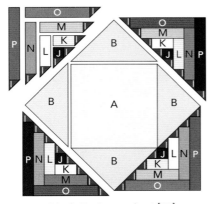

Block Piecing, make 4 [12].

Sash Piecing, make 6 [16].

## Adding Appliqué to the Blocks

1 Using a method of your choice, prepare the C–H patches (page 68) and the strips for appliqué. Cut each bias strip in half and each straight-grain strip into 4 pieces of equal length.

2 Fold a pieced block in half both ways as shown and crease the folds for placement guides. Aligning the folds on the dotted lines of the appliqué design and matching centers, trace the partial block appliqué in each of the 4 sections of the block.

3 Position and blindstitch the leaves and stems on the pieced block. Tuck all leaves under the stems, except those at the ends of the short stems. Appliqué the remaining patches in alphabetical order. Repeat for all the blocks.

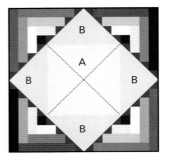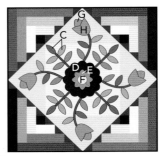

Appliqué Placement

## Assembling the Top

1 Join the blocks and sashes as shown to make the Row 2's.

Row 2, make 2 [4].

2 Beginning with Row 1 and alternating types, join the rows.

3 To add the squared border, sew the strips first to the sides of the quilt. Trim excess length. Add the top and bottom strips in the same way.

• = I ⋆ = R

Row 1, make 3 [5].

Wall quilt/topper is shown in darker colors.
Double comforter includes the complete diagram.

# QUILTING AND FINISHING

**1** To mark the border quilting, follow the Quilting Placement diagram for the size you are making. Beginning in the center of each strip, align the motif or its reverse as shown and mark the border to fill. Mark the blossom in each corner where the motifs meet.

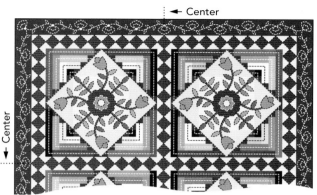

Quilting Placement for Wall Quilt/Topper

**2** Layer the backing, the batting, and the quilt top. Baste them together.

## TIP

Instead of pin or thread basting, you can use a quilt basting spray, which works well in holding the layers of the wall quilt sandwich together for machine quilting.

**3** Quilt the B's, Q's, and the appliqué patches in the ditch as shown and quilt a line through the middle of each log. Quilt the borders as marked.

**4** Bind the quilt. Hand sew a sleeve to the backing of the wall quilt for display.

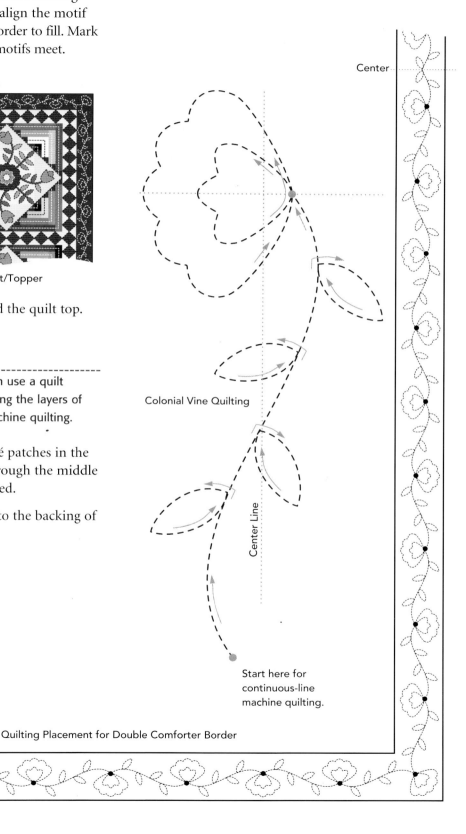

Colonial Vine Quilting

Start here for continuous-line machine quilting.

Quilting Placement for Double Comforter Border

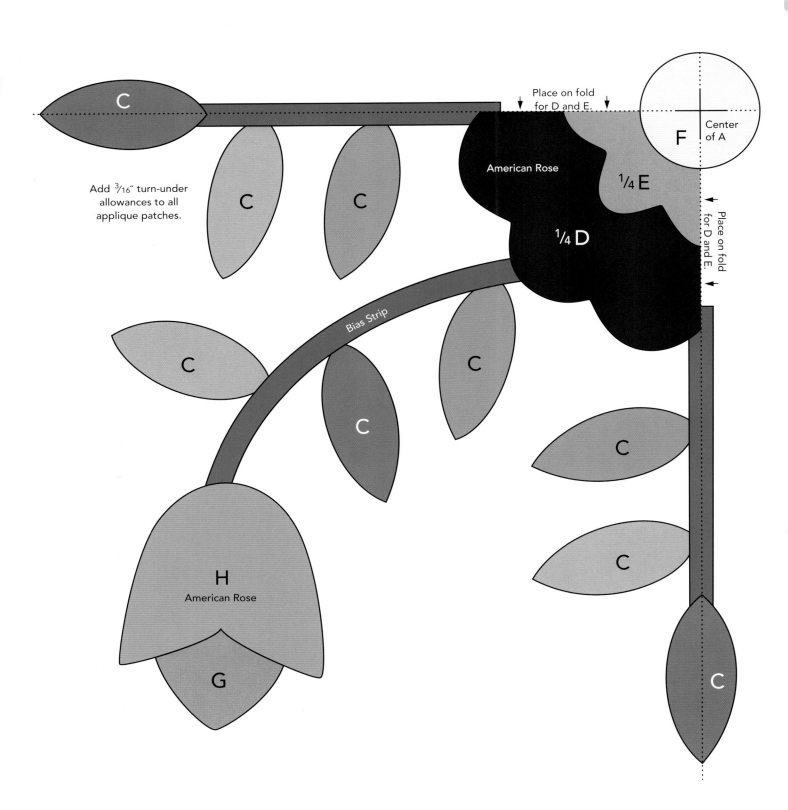

Place on fold for D and E.

American Rose

Center of A

$\frac{1}{4}$ E

$\frac{1}{4}$ D

Place on fold for D and E.

F

C

Add $\frac{3}{16}$″ turn-under allowances to all applique patches.

C

C

C

Bias Strip

C

C

C

C

H

American Rose

G

C

**Made by Anne Olsen, Laramie, Wyoming.
Owned by Rocky Mountain Quilt Museum,
Golden, Colorado.**

A 1995 purchase of partial blocks gave Anne Olsen of Laramie, Wyoming, the opportunity to improve on the accuracy of the original seamstress. Anne added authentic and reproduction 1930s fabrics and many hours of hand-piecing and quilting, transforming those lonely blocks into the splendid quilt you see today.

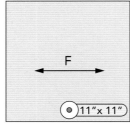

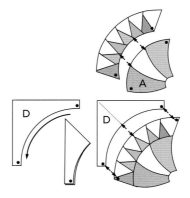

## MATERIALS AND CUTTING

| QUILT SIZE: | Double Comforter |
| --- | --- |
| | 80" × 90½" |
| **BLOCK SIZE:** | |
| 10½" | |
| **YARDAGE:** (44" fabric) | |
| **Cream Solid** | 5⅛ yards |
| | 168 A, 672 C, 112 D, 184 G |
| **Yellow Solid** | ⅛ yard |
| | 28 E |
| **Green Solid** | 4 yards |
| double-fold binding | 10 at 2¼" × 38" |
| | 28 F, 4 H |
| **Prints** | 24 at ¼ yard |
| from each fabric | 7 A, 28 B, 8 G |
| **Backing** | 7½ yards |
| panels | 3 at 33" × 84" |
| **Batting** | 84" × 95" |

For the foundation-piecing option, do not cut the patches listed in colored type. You may need additional yardage.

## ABOUT THIS QUILT

*For help with all phases of the quiltmaking process, including foundation piecing, see Quilting Basics (pages 74–78).*

To make a quilt like this, vary the placement of the prints so that all the blocks are slightly different. You will have 12 extra G patches to put aside for your next scrap quilt.

F

⊙ 11"x 11"

Align arrows with lengthwise or crosswise grain of fabric.

## MAKING THE ARCS

You can either patch piece or foundation piece the arcs for this quilt. For either method, transfer the placement dots to help match end points and seamlines when joining patches and sewn sections.

**To patch piece** the arcs, join B's and C's as shown.

**For foundation piecing,** make 112 copies of the foundation (page 73). Following the numerical order, sew the arcs. Trim on the outer line of each foundation.

Arc Patch Piecing, make 112.

Foundation Arc, make 112.

## THE PINNING PLACE

Pinning first in the middle of curved seams and working outward to the ends helps make a smooth and well-matched seam. When joining the A unit to the arc, pin at the points shown to match the seams. Then align the dots at the ends.

Before joining the D to that unit, fold the curved edge of D in half. Finger press the fold. Match and pin where shown at midcurve and at both ends.

## ASSEMBLING THE BLOCKS AND ROWS

**1** See *The Pinning Place* (page 70), for help sewing curved seams. Join the patches and the arcs to make 28 blocks. Carefully remove the foundation papers if necessary. Appliqué an E patch to the center of each block.

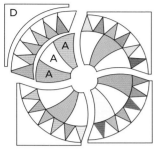

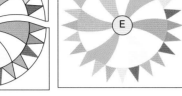

Block Piecing, make 28.

Appliqué Placement

**2** Referring to the diagram below, join the blocks and F patches in rows. Join the rows.

## ADDING THE PIECED BORDER

**1** Join 49 cream and 48 print G's for each side border strip. For each top and bottom strip, join 43 cream and 42 print G's; then add H patches to the ends.

**2** Beginning and ending the stitches ¼" from the ends, sew the side strips to the quilt. Repeat for the top and bottom strips. Join the H and G at each corner to complete the border.

## QUILTING AND FINISHING

**1** Fold a 10½" square sheet of tracing paper in half both ways. Open up and trace the **¼ Plume Thistle Quilting** (page 73) in each section. Fold each F in half both ways and lightly crease. Matching guidelines to the creases, transfer the motifs.

**2** Layer and baste together the backing, the batting, and the quilt top. Outline quilt the patches in the blocks and border as shown, then quilt the marked motifs.

**3** Bind the quilt.

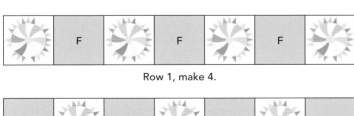

Row 1, make 4.

Row 2, make 4.

Quilting Placement

Side Border, make 2.

Top/Bottom Border, make 2.

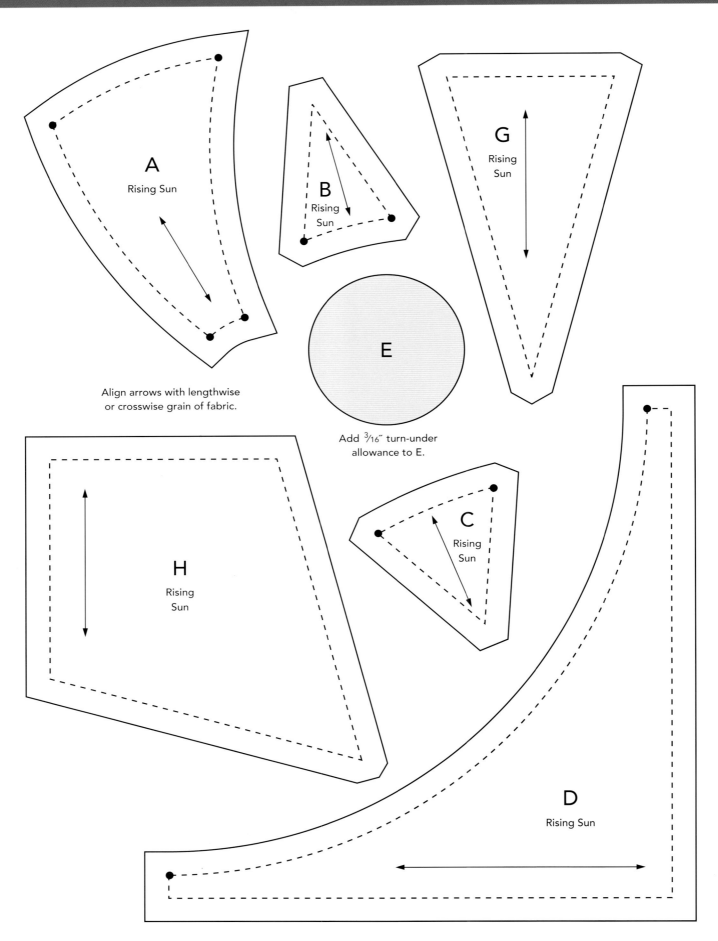

A
Rising Sun

B
Rising Sun

G
Rising Sun

E

Add ³⁄₁₆˝ turn-under allowance to E.

Align arrows with lengthwise or crosswise grain of fabric.

H
Rising Sun

C
Rising Sun

D
Rising Sun

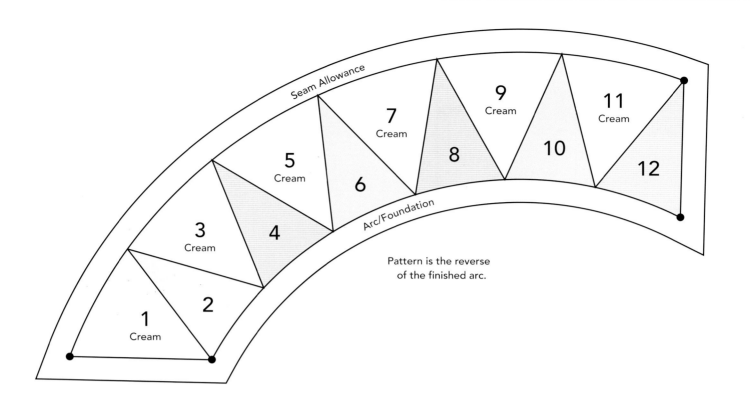

Seam Allowance

Arc/Foundation

| | | | | |
|---|---|---|---|---|
| 9 Cream | 11 Cream | | | |

7 Cream

5 Cream

3 Cream

1 Cream

2

4

6

8

10

12

Pattern is the reverse
of the finished arc.

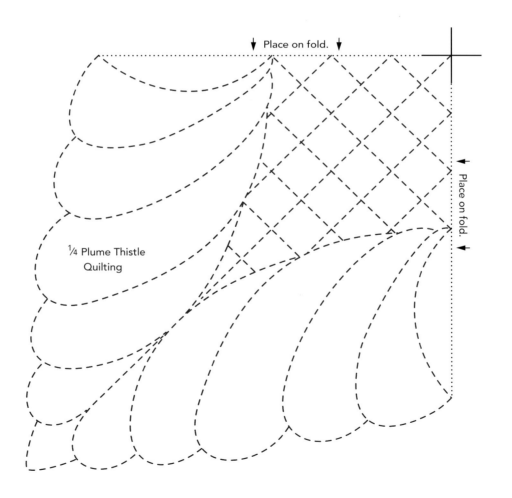

↓ Place on fold. ↓

Place on fold. →

1/4 Plume Thistle
Quilting

# Quilting basics

We use the term "patches" to describe the various pieces of fabric that are sewn together to make a block or a quilt top.

Using a rotary cutter, mat, and an acrylic ruler, cut the shape to the size indicated in the cutting list.

We provide patterns for full-size templates for patches that cannot be easily rotary cut.

Templates for reversed patches are represented with an "r" following the pattern's letter. Turn the template over before marking, or fold fabric wrong sides together when rotary cutting to cut an equal number of patches (A's) and their reverses (Ar's).

If we give half of the pattern piece, the center line is indicated with a dotted line. When making the template, trace around the pattern, flip the tracing over, and align the dotted center lines. Trace around the pattern again to complete the template.

Pressing tabs indicate the direction to press the seam allowances.

Our patterns list finished block sizes, which are typically ½" smaller than unfinished block sizes because they do not include seam allowances.

## BASIC QUILTING SUPPLIES

- Rotary cutter and mat
- Acrylic ruler: Many shapes and sizes are available; a good one to start with is 6" × 24" with ¼" and ⅛" markings
- Scissors: A separate pair for paper and for fabric
- Sewing machine
- ¼" foot
- Walking foot
- Darning foot
- Pins
- Ironing board and iron
- Marking pencils, markers, and so on
- Needles
- Thimble
- Safety pins
- Template plastic
- Thread

The way you mark, cut, and sew varies significantly from machine piecing to hand piecing, so please refer to the appropriate section before starting a project. We recommend that you cut and sew one block using your preferred method before cutting the rest.

## PREPARING YOUR FABRIC

We recommend that you prewash your fabrics. A shrinkage factor is included in our yardage computations.

## MACHINE PIECING

It is important to cut accurately and to sew exact ¼" seams.

### Templates
Trace the patterns on template plastic and cut out accurately.

### Planning
1 Measure, mark, and cut the binding and border strips before cutting patches from the same fabric. Cut larger patches before smaller ones. For best use of the fabric, arrange patches with cutting lines close or touching.

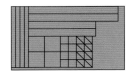

## TRIMMING TEMPLATE

To ensure accurate piecing of triangular patches, you may want to trim the points on patches with 45° angles. Make a template from the full-size trimming template pattern shown here. Align the edges of the trimming template with the patch and trim each point. You may only need to align one of the trimmed sides with the adjacent patch before sewing.

Trimming Template

**2** One or more straight sides of the patch should follow the lengthwise (parallel to the selvages) or crosswise (perpendicular to the selvages) grain of fabric, especially the sides that will be on the outside edges of the quilt block. We indicate lengthwise or crosswise grain with an arrow on the pattern piece.

## Cutting

**1** To find the grainline of your fabric for rotary cutting, hold the fabric with selvages parallel in front of you. Keeping the selvages together, slide the edge closest to you to one side or the other until the fabric hangs straight, without wrinkles or folds. Then lay the fabric down on your cutting mat and cut perpendicular to the fold line. Use this cut edge as your straight-of-grain line.

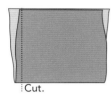
Cut.

**2** Many patches can be cut from strips of fabric by rotary cutting. First, cut a strip of fabric the width needed. Then, cross-cut strips into patches.

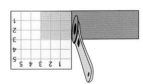

**3** To cut from a template, place the template face down on the wrong side of the fabric and trace with a sharp pencil. Reverse (r) templates should be placed face up on the wrong side of the fabric before tracing.

## Piecing

**1** Align the cut edges of fabric with the edge of the presser foot if it is ¼″ wide. If not, place masking tape on the throat plate of your machine ¼″ away from the needle to guide you. Sew all the way to the cut edge unless you are inserting a patch into an angle (set-in patch).

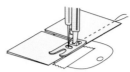

**2** A set-in patch is inserted in an angle formed by 2 other patches. First, mark the seamlines on all 3 patches so you'll know exactly where to stitch. Align the edges of 2 patches and pin along the marked lines. Sew the seam, stopping the stitches at the end of the marked seamline; backstitch. Pivot the set-in patch so the adjacent edge aligns with the edge of the third patch. Matching seams, pin in place.

**3** Starting exactly where the previous seam ended, sew 2 stitches, then backstitch, taking care not to stitch into the seam allowance. Stitch to the outer edge.

## HAND PIECING

### Templates and Cutting Patches

**1** Mark the seamlines, rather than cutting lines, when hand piecing. Cut out patches approximately ¼″ beyond the marked seamlines.

**2** To make a template for hand piecing, trace the seamline (dashed) of a full-size template pattern on template plastic. To convert rotary cutting diagrams to hand-piecing templates, first draw the shape to scale, then subtract ¼″ from every side. Trace the full-size templates on the wrong side of your fabric using a sharp pencil, leaving at least ½″ between each traced line.

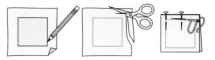

## Piecing

Put patches right sides together, matching seamlines. Sew the seam through the marked lines with a short running stitch using a single thread. Begin and end stitching at the seamline (not the edge of the fabric) with two or three backstitches to secure the seam.

Running Stitch     Backstitch

## FOUNDATION PIECING

**1** Make paper copies of each foundation. Sew patches in the numerical order printed on the pattern. Center fabric under #1, wrong side of the fabric to the unprinted side of the paper, and pin in place from the paper side.

**2** Turn fabric side up. With right sides together, position a patch of fabric sufficient to cover #2 and its seam allowances so the fabric's edge extends at least ¼″ into the #2 area. Pin in place. Set a very short stitch length on your sewing machine (18–20 per inch or 1.5 mm).

**3** Turn the assembly paper side up. Stitch through the paper and the fabric layers along the printed seamline, beginning and ending ¼″ beyond the ends of the line.

**4** Turn the assembly to the fabric side. Trim the seam allowances to approximately ¼″. Press the fabric open to cover #2 and the seam allowances.

**5** Repeat this process to complete the blocks or sections, allowing at least ¼″ beyond the edge of the paper.

**6** Use a rotary cutter and ruler to trim ¼″ outside the seamline of the foundation, creating a seam allowance. If necessary, join sections by matching points and sewing with ¼″ seam. Once all the seams around a foundation section have been sewn, remove the paper foundations.

## APPLIQUÉ

No turn-under allowances are given on appliqué patterns.

Using a light table if needed, position background fabric over the appliqué placement diagram. Lightly mark the major shapes with pencil or chalk. Optionally, finger crease the fabric in half lengthwise, crosswise, and diagonally to form guidelines for placement of the patches.

### Turned-Edge Appliqué

**1** It is helpful to have as many bias edges as possible on the perimeter of your appliqué patches. Trace and cut on the seamline of the pattern to make a template. Place the template face up on the right side of the fabric (face down on the right side for a reverse patch) and lightly draw around it. Cut out each patch about ³⁄₁₆″ outside the marked line.

**2** On inward curves, clip the ³⁄₁₆″ allowances almost to the marked seamline. Turn under the allowance and finger press.

**3** Pin or baste appliqué patches on the background fabric. To appliqué by hand, use a blind stitch and a thread color that matches the patch. To appliqué by machine, use a small zigzag or blind hem stitch and monofilament thread.

**4** If the background fabric shows through the appliquéd patch, carefully cut away the background fabric to within ³⁄₁₆″ of the appliqué patch or use 2 layers of appliqué fabric.

### Bias Strips

Bias strips are cut at a 45° angle to the grain of the fabric. They are stretchy and therefore ideal for creating curved appliqué stems.

**1** Make your first cut by aligning a 45° guideline on your acrylic ruler with the cut edge or selvage of your fabric. Use this new bias edge to cut strips the required width.

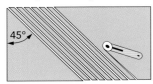

**2** Prepare bias strips for appliqué by folding in half lengthwise, wrong sides together. Stitch ¼″ from the fold. Offset the seam allowance; press toward the center. Trim the seam allowance to ⅛″.

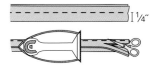

## PRESSING

Press all seam allowances to one side, usually toward the darker fabric; follow the pressing tabs presented with each pattern. When joining blocks and/or rows, seam allowances are pressed to allow nesting of seams. This reduces bulk in the quilt top.

## BORDERS

### Squared Borders

**1** Squared borders are added first to the sides of the quilt center, then to the top and bottom. Measure through the vertical center of quilt top from raw edge to raw edge and mark this length with pins on the side border strips.

**2** Matching pins, fold the strips in half and lightly crease to mark the centers of the border strips. Fold the quilt top in half to mark the centers of its sides. Matching marked centers and matching the pins to the quilt ends, sew the side border strips to the quilt. Trim any extra border length and press.

**3** To add the top and bottom border strips, measure through the horizontal center of the quilt top, including the side borders, and repeat this procedure.

### Mitered Borders

**1** Mitered borders are added by sewing border strips to all sides of the quilt center, and then mitering each corner. Measure the vertical and horizontal centers of the quilt and mark edges and border strips as described above. When joining each border strip to the quilt, begin and end stitches 1/4" from the quilt top corners and backstitch.

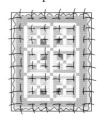

**2** Referring to the diagrams, fold the quilt top right sides together at one corner. Fold the border/quilt seam allowances toward the quilt top, match seamlines, and pin through both layers about 3" from the corner.

**3** Place a ruler along the folded edge of the quilt top, intersecting the final stitch in the border seam and extending through the border strip. Draw a line from the stitch to the outer edge of the border.

**4** Align long raw edges of the borders and pin together along the pencil line.

**5** Sew along the line to the edge of the border; backstitch. Trim seam allowances to 1/4"; press open. Repeat for all corners.

## MARKING

Trace the quilting motif on tracing paper. Place the tracing paper under the quilt top with a light source behind it. Lightly mark the design on the quilt top with a hard lead pencil or a marker of your choice. Test any marking product for removability before using it on your quilt.

Straight lines may be "marked" as you quilt by using masking tape that is pulled away after quilting along its edge.

## BACKING AND BASTING

Make the quilt backing 4"–8" larger than the quilt top. Remove the selvages to avoid puckers. Usually two or three lengths must be sewn together. Press the seam allowances open. Place the backing wrong side up on a flat surface, stretch slightly, and tape or pin in place. Smooth the batting over the backing. Center the quilt top right side up on top of the batting. Pin the layers as necessary to secure them while basting.

### Basting for Machine Quilting

Machine-quilted tops can be basted with rustproof safety pins. Begin at the center and place pins 3" to 4" apart, avoiding lines to be quilted.

### Basting for Hand Quilting

Beginning in the center of the quilt, baste horizontal and vertical lines 4" to 6" apart.

## QUILTING

Quilt in the ditch refers to quilting right next to the seamline on the side without seam allowances. Outline quilting refers to quilting 1/4" from the seamline.

### Machine Quilting

Before machine quilting, bring bobbin thread to the top of the quilt so it doesn't get caught as you quilt: lower presser foot, hold the top thread and take one stitch down and up, lift the presser foot to release the thread tension, and tug on the top thread to draw a loop of the bobbin thread to the top of the quilt. Pull the bobbin thread to the top. Lower the needle into the same hole created by the initial stitch, lower your presser foot, and start quilting. A walking foot is used for straight-line or ditch quilting. To free-motion quilt, drop (or cover) your feed dogs and use a darning foot. Start and end your quilting lines with 1/4" of very short stitches to secure.

### Hand Quilting

Hand quilting is done in a short running stitch with a single strand of thread that goes through all three layers.

Use a short needle (8 or 9 between) with about 18" of thread. Make a small knot in the thread, and take a long first stitch (about 1") through the top and batting only, coming up where the quilting will begin. Tug on the thread to pull the knotted end between the layers. Take short, even stitches that are the same size on the top and back of the quilt. Push the needle with a thimble on your middle finger. Guide the fabric in front of the needle with the thumb of one hand above the quilt and with the middle finger of your other hand under the quilt.

To end a line of quilting, make a small knot in the thread close to the quilt top, push the needle through the top and batting only, and bring it to the surface about 1″ away. Tug the thread until the knot pulls through the quilt top, burying the knot in the batting. Clip the thread close to the surface of the quilt.

## BINDING

**1** Baste around the quilt ³⁄₁₆″ from the edges. Trim the batting and backing ¼″ beyond the edge of the quilt top.

**2** To prepare the binding strips, place the ends of 2 binding strips perpendicular to each other, right sides together. Stitch diagonally and trim to ¼″. In this way, join all the strips and press the seam allowances open.

**3** Cut the beginning of the binding strip at a 45° angle. Fold the binding strip in half along the length, wrong sides together, and press.

Starting in the middle of a side and leaving a 6″ tail of binding loose, align the raw edges of the binding with the edge of the quilt top. Begin sewing the binding to the quilt using a ¼″ seam allowance. Stop ¼″ from the first corner; backstitch. Remove the needle from the quilt and cut the threads.

**4** Fold the binding up, then back down even with the edge of the quilt. Begin stitching ¼″ from the binding fold, backstitch to secure, and continue sewing. Repeat at all corners.

**5** When nearing the starting point, leave at least 12″ of the quilt edge unbound and a 10″–12″ binding tail. Smooth the beginning tail over the ending tail. Following the cut edge of the beginning tail, draw a line on the ending tail at a 45° angle.

**6** To add a seam allowance, draw a cutting line ½″ out from the first line. Make sure it guides you to cut the binding tail ½″ longer than the first line. Cut on this second line.

**7** To join the ends, place them right sides together. Offset the points so the strips match ¼″ in from the edge and sew. Press the

seam allowances open. Press the section of binding in half and then finish sewing it to the quilt. Trim away excess backing and batting in the corners only to eliminate bulk.

**8** Fold the binding to the back of the quilt, enclosing the extra batting and backing. Blindstitch the binding fold to the backing, just covering the previous line of stitching.

## SLEEVE FOR HANGING

**1** Sleeve edges can be caught in the seam when you sew the binding to the quilt. Cut the strip(s) listed in the pattern and join for the length needed.

**2** Press allowances to one side.

**3** Hem the short ends of the sleeve by folding under ½″, pressing, then folding and pressing once more; topstitch close to the edge of the hem.

**4** Fold the sleeve in half lengthwise, wrong sides together, matching raw edges.

**5** Center the sleeve on the back and top of the quilt and baste.

**6** Sew the binding to the quilt. Once the binding has been sewn, smooth the sleeve against the backing and blindstitch along the bottom and along the ends of the sleeve, catching some of the batting in the stitches.

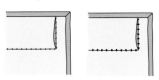

# Resources

For a list of other fine books from C&T Publishing, ask for a free catalog:

C&T Publishing, Inc.
P.O. Box 1456
Lafayette, CA 94549
(800) 284-1114
Email: ctinfo@ctpub.com
Website: www.ctpub.com

For quilting supplies:

Cotton Patch
1025 Brown Ave.
Lafayette, CA 94549
(800) 835-4418 or
(925) 283-7883
Email: CottonPa@aol.com
Website: www.quiltusa.com

Note: Fabrics used in the quilts shown may not be currently available, as fabric manufacturers keep most fabrics in print for only a short time.

C&T Publishing's professional photography services are now available to the public. Visit us at www.ctmediaservices.com

For subscriptions to *Quiltmaker* or to purchase back issues, patterns, quilting stencils or quilting motif books and CDs:
Website: quiltmaker.com
Website: VillageQuiltshoppe.com
Email: customercare@quiltmaker.com

*Quiltmaker*
741 Corporate Circle, Suite A
Golden, CO 80401
(800) 881–6634 ext. 5644
(303) 215–5644

# About the Author

*Quiltmaker* magazine has been providing quilters with patterns for a wide variety of quilts since 1982. Founded by Bonnie Leman as a sister magazine to *Quilter's Newsletter Magazine*, it offers creative designs for quilters of all levels, in sizes from crib to king.

*Quiltmaker* is known for step-by-step instructions that include quick and easy techniques, full-size templates, and rotary-cutting diagrams. Under the direction of Editor-in-Chief Brenda Bauermeister Groelz, *Quiltmaker* continues to please its readers with fresh patterns in up-to-date fabrics.

*Quiltmaker* magazine is a publication of CK Media. For more about *Quiltmaker*, visit their website at quiltmaker.com.